Now That Nursing Orientation Is Over

The Professional Experiences of

Jean McGrath-Brown,

RN, MA, LNHA

Jean McGrath-Brown, RN, MA, LNHA

Kravitz & Sons

INNOVATORS IN PUBLISHING, MARKETING AND ADVERTISING

Kravitz and Sons LLC
204 E Arlington Blvd. Suite B
Greenville, NC 27858

Published by Kravitz and Sons LLC.

ISBN: 979-8-89639-510-2 (sc)
ISBN: 979-8-89639-511-9 (e)

Library of Congress Control Number: 2025918598

Now That Nursing Orientation Is Over

The Professional Experiences of
Jean McGrath-Brown
RN, MA, LNHA

Jean McGrath-Brown, RN, MA, LNHA

This book is dedicated to Sister Victoria for her
kindness and understanding in giving me a chance and
for her contributions to the nursing profession.

Daughters of Charity
2800 Main Street
Bridgeport, Ct 06606

SISTER VICTORIA NOLAN, DC

RESUME

Education –

B.S. in Nursing – Catholic University, Washington, D.C.
M.S. in Nursing - Catholic University, Washington, D.C.
Certified Chaplain in Pastoral Ministry, National Association
           of Catholic Chaplains authorized by the
           United States Catholic Conference.

Experience –

General Education, Instructor   9 years

Nursing
    Director, Nursing Service/education   19 years

Parish Ministry
    Director, Parish Center which included
    development of a Neighborhood Health Center   3 years

Community Development
    Associate Director of Ethnic/racial Affairs,
    Cardinal's Commission on Human Relations,
    Archdiocese of Philadelphia   8 years

Health Education
    Director, Health Education, Lourdes Hospital   3 years

Pastoral Ministry
    Director, Pastoral Care Department, Lourdes   10 years
    Chaplain, in Pastoral Ministry – St. Vincent's Medical Ctr. 15 years
    Presently retired – a volunteer in Pastoral Care Dept. 20 hours
    Retired to St. Louise House May 2, 2009 a week

Membership
    Certified Chaplain, Emeritus – National Association of
    Catholic Chaplains
    Member of Institutional Review Board-St Vincent Med. Ctr.

Aunt Tilly—Ms. Grace Bryan-Spence, RN.

Table of Contents

Foreword: About the Author

Jean McGrath, RN, MA, LNHA, was born in Darliston, Westmoreland, Jamaica, in the West Indies. She immigrated to the United States in 1967, and thanks to Sister Victoria, director of St. Mary's Hospital School of Nursing, in Rochester, New York, she was admitted into their three-year nursing program. This gave Ms. McGrath the opportunity to fulfill her lifelong dream of becoming a nurse. She was first inspired by her aunt Tilly at the age of twelve when she visited her at the University of the West Indies while she was caring for a patient with a leg wound in the emergency room. She was dressed in her white cap and white starched uniform. Ms. McGrath made her decision then as to what her life's work would be.

On June 13, 1971, Ms. McGrath graduated from St. Mary's with the distinguished Alumni Association Award. Her graduating class of thirty-four would be the last class to graduate from the school. St. Mary's first opened its doors in 1892, with the first class graduation in 1894. Seventy-nine years later, on June 13, 1971, with Ms. Virginia Krenzer as the school's director, and with a total of 1,983 graduates, St. Mary's closed its nursing school.

In June 1982, Ms. McGrath received her bachelor of arts degree, majoring in business management, from Mary Mount Manhattan College, on East Seventy-First Street in New York City. In June 2004, twenty-two years later, she received her master of arts degree, majoring in urban affairs, from Queens College, City University of New York. Three years later, in the fall of 2007, she received her nursing home administrator's license in Tallahassee, Florida.

With more than thirty-eight years of experience as a nurse leader, and licensed in four states, Ms. McGrath brings a wide breadth of knowledge and experience in her contribution to *Now That Nursing Orientation Is Over*. She held various positions in her long career at well-known institutions. After graduation, she worked in the intensive care unit at St. Mary's Hospital in Rochester, New York, as a staff nurse, and then she moved to New York City to be near her family. She settled in Queens, New York, and worked at Booth Memorial Hospital, now known as New York Hospital of Queens, as a staff nurse. She left there to work at Fairview Nursing Home, a two-hundred-bed skilled care facility, as a nursing supervisor. She then obtained a position at Queens Hospital Center, a twelve-hundred-bed teaching hospital in Jamaica, New York, on the surgical service as nurse clinician/ nursing supervisor. Ms. McGrath was later promoted to become one of the administrative nursing supervisors on the evening tour (3 to 11 p.m.), covering several units in "A" building, as it was called then. She worked with several assistant directors of nursing there, who found her to be dependable, committed, and able to handle high-level assignments, which included providing administrative coverage for half of the hospital on the weekends. These were all acute care services. She served as an acting nursing administrator for the assistant director of nursing on the 3 to 11 p.m. tour covering the whole hospital for a short time. Ms. McGrath had great responsibility placed upon her in this role, in which she not only met the standards of the organization, but exceeded their expectations. Later she worked at a nursing home in Woodmere, New York, as an assistant director of nursing. When the director retired, she was offered the position of director of nursing, but she declined because she had her own business at the time. Ms. McGrath had her own nursing agency, Nightingale Nursing Registry, in Jamaica, New York. There, she supplied registered nurses (RNs) and licensed practical nurses (LPNs) to nursing homes and nursing assistants to private homes.

She then worked at Mount Sinai Medical Center, a twelve-hundred-bed teaching hospital in New York City. First, she worked as a surgical admission planner scheduling surgeries for the hospital, and then as a home care coordinator. While in the position of coordinator, she received a commendation during the exit interview from a state visit in 1991. She also worked as a per diem nurse and a private duty nurse. She spent over twenty years at this hospital. She also worked as a guardian appointed by Justice of the Supreme Court of New York County Diane A. Lebedeff, to supervise and care for an incapacitated person. She was given full powers to care for and to place her ward in an appropriate facility that met her medical and social needs.

In June 2004, after receiving her master's degree in urban affairs, she moved to Florida. She worked at a long-term rehabilitation hospital on Las Olas Boulevard in Fort Lauderdale as an administrative nursing supervisor covering the whole hospital (7 p.m. to 7 a.m.). Then she worked at 180-bed facility and, after that, at another skilled care facility as a risk manager/ nursing supervisor. She spent one year as an administrator in training (AIT) in a skilled care facility under the leadership of the executive director in Broward County, Florida. After successful completion of state and nation examinations, she received her nursing home administrator's license in the fall of 2007. In 2008, she became director of nursing for a short time at a small rehab hospital before moving back to New York. There she worked in the Bronx at a 240-bed skilled care facility as the administrative nursing supervisor on the 3 to 11 p.m. tour. Ms. McGrath now resides in Florida with her family.

Acknowledgments

First, I would like to thank God for his many blessings over my life. Thanks to my wonderful daughters, Jo, Susie, and Jackie; my husband, Anthony; my granddaughters, Taylor and Ashley; and my son-in-law, Kenton, who encouraged me with my work. Thanks to Vivien, who initially assisted me with typing.

To Jackie Singletary, I express my gratitude and appreciation for her patience in word processing the book and for her editing assistance as we went along. As she is a published author, her suggestions were invaluable to me.

Introduction

Nursing is a noble profession, and nurses everywhere are special people who give of themselves tirelessly. Nurses experience a stark contrast from school to the floors after having learned the art and science of nursing in the classroom. Nurses everywhere are sometimes shocked at the true reality of what patient care involves. Nurses are hardworking—there is no question about that. You see them walking back and forth in the halls of hospitals and nursing homes taking care of patients. They endure a lot from the patients, their families, the doctors, their coworkers, and their superiors. There are set nursing standards that have to be adhered to in order to be in compliance with the state and the institution they work for. Over the span of my career, I have experienced great joy and satisfaction in what I do for a living, knowing that I have impacted the lives of others in a practical way. I reflect on the lives I helped to save, knowing that understanding, compassion, and kindness were always uttermost in my mind and that I did the best I could at all times ... even when I was tired, weary, and on my way home.

It is not only the big things that count but also the small things, such as a smiling face, giving assurance, speaking softly to the patients, and taking time to listen to patients. These things show the patient that you care and want to help. Listening to a patient can help save lives and bring comfort to a soul. Making a phone call for a patient—even if the patient is confused—putting on a pair of socks when they complain that their feet are cold, sitting with them for a few minutes when they can't sleep, fluffing up a pillow, giving an extra warm blanket, and turning off a television are just a few of the many things that nurses do aside from their routine nursing care. Nurses everywhere are assets to human society. They improve and change the lives of their patients. Nurses work hard continually, always putting the patients first. As stressful and demanding as their work may be at times, most nurses you speak to will tell you how they enjoy what they do. They go home and are able to sleep knowing that they have done their best.

Nurses need to be recognized and commended for the godly work that they do every day saving and improving the lives of their patients. They are dedicated professionals with a mission to heal the sick. Nursing is definitely a calling. It is much more than a profession. It is a calling from God to care for and heal the sick. It calls for kindness, patience, empathy, understanding, and devotion. I knew when I was a young girl, as I watched my aunt Tilly in the emergency room at the University of the West Indies, caring for a patient with an ulcer on his lower leg, that I wanted to be a nurse. She was wearing a starched white uniform with an apron and a white cap. Her smile was radiant, reassuring, and beautiful. She was so kind and gentle as she cared for her patient. She looked like an angel! At that moment, I was deeply moved and inspired by her love for another human being. It was that day that I knew in my heart what I wanted my life's work to be.

As Sister Victoria, my beloved mentor and the director of St. Mary's Hospital School of Nursing in Rochester, New York (1963 to 1969), said in her June 1969 commencement speech,

You and I were put on this earth, as God tells us, not to leave things the way they are but to transform the world ... so that it will bear a mark of his intelligence and his concern. You are living in an age of secular competence. No nurse really fulfills her obligations unless she is at least striving to attain the measure of competence her innate talents permit. A nurse cannot be satisfied to drift throughout twenty, thirty, or forty years of service on her basic education, whatever it is or was. As a matter of justice and of Christian duty, you must keep abreast of new knowledge and spend yourselves in applying what you learn.

Nurses are God's angels. They transform the lives of their patients on a daily basis. Whether you are a new graduate, an experienced nurse, a nurse starting in a new area of the wide profession of nursing, or a nurse coming from a different country or state, once the classroom orientation is over and the reality of the job sets in, it can be very challenging and even overwhelming at times. The nurse is expected to do so much, constantly multitasking, prioritizing, and assessing and reassessing the situation while evaluating the needs and care of the patient.

This book is informational. It is based on a compilation of experiences I gained over thirty-eight years in the nursing profession, working at several institutions and holding different titles as a nurse. I started after graduation as an ICU nurse at St. Mary's Hospital in Rochester, New York. I also worked as a medical surgical nurse on a very busy orthopedic floor, with patients going and coming from surgery. I then worked as a nursing supervisor in a two-hundred-bed nursing home, and then as a clinician/nursing supervisor in a twelve-hundred-bed acute care city hospital. I then worked as an assistant director of nursing in a nursing home I was president and CEO of my own nursing agency, and an acting nurse administrator on the 3 to 11 p.m. tour covering an entire hospital for a short time, where I started as a nurse clinician on the day tour. Then a few years later, I worked only on the weekends covering half of a hospital on the day tour. I became a surgical admission planner in another twelve-hundred-bed hospital in New York City. In addition, I worked as a private duty nurse, a per diem nurse, and a home care coordinator. I spent over twenty years at that hospital. I moved from New York and worked as an administrative supervisor in a rehab long-term care hospital in

Florida on the night tour, in charge of the entire hospital. I then worked in a skilled care 180-bed facility as a nursing supervisor and later in another skilled care 120-bed facility as a supervisor/risk manager. I interned as an administrator in training (AIT). I worked as director of nursing in a small rehabilitation hospital for a short time, and once again in New York as an administrative nursing supervisor on the 3 to 11 p.m. tour, covering a 240-bed skilled care facility.

The Experience of Nursing

Most of my nursing experience has been in the state of New York. First, I worked in Rochester. Then I moved four hundred miles away to live near my family in Queens, New York. I worked in Queens, then in New York City, and then in the Bronx. The rest of my experience has been in the state of Florida, where I currently am a licensed nursing home administrator.

To begin with, a nurse wears many caps. S/he is required to be of high caliber and to be able to assess situations quickly and make prudent decisions that result in saving lives. S/he has to be able to multitask, prioritize and make split-second decisions, always thinking of the patients first. S/he is the person on the floor that the doctors and the entire health-care team go to for information. S/he has to be mentally alert at all times, know her/his patients well, and do whatever is necessary at the moment to preserve the patients' lives and keep them safe. Patients depend on the nurse, and s/he always has to perform at her/his very best, caring for all of her/his patients as if they were her/his parents or family members. I spoke with a nurse recently who works in the emergency room, and she said that her experience so far has been a good one. She was given three months to complete her orientation. She has a preceptor and clinician and feels that she is not alone. She can go to the preceptor whenever she is unsure of something, and for this she is grateful. However, I have spoken to nurses who work in the ICU, and they have said that their first days and weeks after orientation in the classroom were not what they had expected. One asked herself if this was what she really had expected: "Is this what I want to do for my life work?" She had no idea that nursing was so stressful or intense. There were times, she said, when nurses were forced to either sink or swim.

Another nurse who works on telemetry said that they gradually broke her in after orientation, and in spite of the critical nature of the unit, she was able to function with help from the other nurses. Now, she said, "I have been here fifteen years strong."

I have spoken to another nurse who told me that she did her practical orientation in a nursing home, and she had twenty- five patients to give medication to. She said that the nurse in charge of those twenty-five patients was right beside her and guided her. However, she felt that this was too stressful and that there were too many patients for her to manage on her own. "I was turned off," she said. Once she graduated, she did not want that type of nursing. She now works in a prison. Her job there holds a different kind of stress, because she always wonders what might go wrong with the prisoners and who might get hurt. In her daily activities, her main assignment is to administer medications and to do daily documentation. She said she is surprised when she sees these docile-looking prisoners lined up for their medications. Many of them look like they couldn't hurt a fly. They are the same ones who are in for murder, rape, and armed robbery. She enjoys her job, but she always has to watch her back.

I have spoken to nurses who have worked on hospice, and they tell me that they enjoy what they do. They enjoy making the patient's end of life more comfortable and serene. I have spoken to nurses who work the night shift in the ER, and they tell me that when they go to work, their greatest fear is that they do not have the regular staff working that know the unit.

Another nurse told me that her greatest fear is never knowing what will bring patients through the door next—whether it's a plane crash, motor vehicle accident, gunshot wound, or severe asthma attack.

Recently, I spoke with some ER nurses. One told me she went into nursing because her mother was sick in the ICU and was getting ready to be transferred to a step-down unit. Before her mother left the unit, she was given a drug and shortly after that she coded and died. Because of this, the daughter decided she wanted to become a nurse. The other ER nurse said that she was so scared the first day she was off orientation. She was working the evening shift, and she had two very sick patients. She said it was only God that helped her. Now, she says, eight years later, "I'm still here." Another ER nurse said that for her it was an easy transition because she worked in the ER as an ER technician prior to becoming a nurse, and she still loves nursing.

What Happens During and After Orientation

When nurses start a new job, they receive an official orientation. The time they spend in orientation varies among hospitals, nursing homes, and assisted living facilities. They are welcomed by the director of services. They are introduced to various department heads of the hospital or the nursing home. Each of them come and speak for an hour or so about the institution and what is expected of you as a new employee. Sometimes the administrator stops in and also welcomes you. They discuss benefits and job descriptions, and you are given a handbook in which everything you learn in orientation is written out in detail. The information includes various services that the hospital or nursing home provides. Its policies and procedures are clear. Later, they take you for a tour on the floor in the facility so you can see what really happens on the floor. Most times, the nurses are very busy, but they often stop to welcome you, hoping that they will be getting more help on their unit.

It is extremely important that a nurse is current with her/his education, and practical application of her/his nursing knowledge, to function effectively. Nursing requires continual education for the nurses to keep up with the latest in their particular fields. In a hospital, the orientation period is much longer than it is in a nursing home. Specialized areas such as the emergency room require orientation periods of as long as three months, depending on your background, experience, and ability to grasp and apply what you have learned.

Once a nurse completes the classroom orientation, s/he is often excited and looks forward to going on the floor. The nurse teams up with a preceptor who is usually experienced, and most times has worked for a while at the institution. A preceptor is recognized by her/his peers and supervisor as a good teacher/educator, able to teach the new nurse the skills necessary to do well on the unit. The nurse is taught how to prioritize, observe, assess, document, and take telephone orders from the doctors. S/he knows the brand and generic names of medications and administers them. S/he is taught time management and the routine for that particular unit. The preceptor assists the nurses in decision making if they are unsure. S/he assesses their strengths and weaknesses and gives helpful suggestions and words of encouragement, while trying not to micromanage their every move. The preceptor works with the nurses until they are able to function independently on the unit. A nurse may work in a specialized unit such as the intensive care unit (ICU), emergency room (ER), the operating room (OR), labor and delivery, the neonatal intensive care unit (NICU), the transplant unit, or the psychiatric unit, to name a few.

In nursing homes, the orientation is much less extensive. To begin with, they are smaller than a hospital, and the units are similar. In most nursing facilities, one or two floors are primarily for rehabilitation patients; that is, patients who recently came from the hospital after a stroke, heart attack, motor vehicle accident (MVA)_, surgery in general, or other reasons, and who must have a structured rehab program to regain their functional ability—or as close as possible to what it was prior to hospitalization. These units are usually for short-term rehabilitation. A majority of these patients are alert and oriented. They are aware that they have had an experience such as knee, hip, abdominal, or bypass surgery. They are aware of fall precautions, hip precautions, dressings that need to be changed, their own limitations, and pain medications. They know the names of the medications and when they were last administered. Other patients in the facility may have various stages of dementia or Alzheimer's and require total nursing care. Some stroke patients, people who have been in motor vehicle accidents, and cardiac patients spend a long time in a nursing facility, depending on the severity of their individual medical needs. The other floors may have a few rehab patients where the long-term patients reside. Long-term residents can range in age from young to very old. An example could be a motor vehicle accident patient with multiple injuries and disabilities. Alzheimer's patients in different stages of the disease rarely get well enough to go home. Dementia patients and patients with terminal illnesses such as cancer, stroke patients, patients with insulin-dependent diabetes mellitus (IDDM), and patients with multiple complications spend a very long time in a nursing home. Many of them die there. Some patients have amputations, diabetic ulcers, or multiple system failure such as end-stage renal disease (ESRD), leukemia, multiple myeloma, and other terminal chronic illnesses. These are some of the many patients who live in nursing homes today.

Nurses can function well on any of these units in nursing homes because of the similarity of the different diagnoses and nursing care needs. This is unlike the hospital, where the units all provide acute care and are specialized, such as ICUs, telemetry, OR, ER, pediatrics, newborn nursery, orthopedic medical units, surgical units, transplant units, cardiothoracic units, oncology units, dialysis units, hospice units, research units, and special procedures, to name a few. Nurses who work in these units all have to be certified to work in these areas.

St. Mary's Hospital, where I went to school, was affiliated with Seton Psychiatric Institute in Baltimore, Maryland, and we spent three months there for our psychiatric training. Our class of 1971 lived and studied on campus. We cared only for psychiatric patients during this rotation. Some patients were Catholic nuns and priests. The experiences were startling initially until I understood the behaviors that were exhibited during group therapy sessions. I learned a great deal but found myself becoming depressed after observing some very sad cases. I wasn't sure if I was helping my patients, even though I tried my best. I was happy to leave after my three months and to return to my dormitory at St. Mary's. I then knew for sure that medical/surgical nursing was my preference. Yet, when I received my State Board of Nursing results, my highest grade was in psychiatry. I never worked in psych as a staff nurse in my later years, but occasionally I would cover the psych units in "T" building, as it used to be called at Queens Hospital Center.

Starting Your Shift

Report is given at the beginning and ending of all shifts. Some hospitals have twelve-hour shifts; others are still eight hours. In some hospitals, the nurses give report at the nursing station and also ask visitors to leave if it is a closed unit such as the ICUs. In other hospitals, the nurses walk to and stand outside a patient's room door as they give report. This gives the nurse coming on duty a visual picture of the patient's condition. They speak softly, taking into consideration the Health Insurance Portability and Accountability Act of 1996 (HIPAA) rules of patient privacy. Other institutions give report in the medication room, where they can speak freely, or at the back nursing station, where the computer is available and they can check certain information and orders as the report is being given. The nurses do not all give report at the same time. This leaves some nurses on the floor with the patient care assistants (PCAs) or certified nursing assistants (CNAs) to answer patient call lights and report emergencies to the nurse.

The unit clerk or secretary has the lists of patients on the floor at her/his desk. S/he knows the nurse and the CNA assigned to each patient, and s/he has the phone number for each nurse. In this way, s/he can call the nurse quickly. In many hospitals today, once the nurses come on duty, they are assigned a telephone to communicate directly with the doctors and family members. They report critical lab values, obtain new orders, and communicate with the pharmacist, just to mention a few of the things they can do with easy access to their telephones.

When the report is completed, the nurses coming on duty makes rounds on all of their patients, doing a quick assessment of them. They follow up on issues of the previous tour. Then they prepare to administer medications, take blood pressures, do glucose testing, and call physicians as needed. They deal with patients and family issues, and they make appropriate, concise, and detailed notes in the computer as various events take place, depending on what's happening on the unit. The charge nurse assigns the nurses and CNAs to their patients. S/he takes into consideration patients' acuity, the nurses' ability, and the number of nurses s/he has to staff the unit. In some cases, some nurses have to "float" from one unit to another if there are sick calls. The charge nurse has to think about continuity of care and the nurses that would be best suited for the patients s/he assigns them to.

Nurses have to take part in on-the-spot emergencies all the time. They call codes, initiate CPR, and administer advanced cardiac life support until the code team arrives. The nurses make sure that the crash cart is checked and the defibrillator, the intubation tube, and all suction, oxygen, and emergency equipment are in working order and are present on the cart. If a code is in progress, as soon as the code is over, the cart has to be sent to the pharmacy to be restocked. If she is working on the day tour, the nurses prepare patients for surgery. They do preoperative teaching with all the patients. They make sure they remain NPO and all the labs, X-rays, and MRIs are on the chart. S/he checks the spelling of the patient's name on his/her name bands because surgery cannot be performed unless the name is spelled correctly. Nurses ask the patients if they have had food or drink since midnight. They get patients ready for special procedures and other tests. They start intravenous lines for IV infusion, or they change sites of existing IVs if the IV is infiltrated. They draw blood, do stat electrocardiograms (EKGs), and give stat IV medications and antibiotics. They interact with the multidisciplinary team who care for the patients.

Nursing administrators; the chief nursing officer; the directors of various services such as ICU medical surgical units and telemetry; and heads of each department attend the morning meetings. They discuss outstanding events that took place overnight in the hospital, especially regarding the emergency room, emergency surgeries, deaths, falls with injuries, admissions, family/patient complaints, unannounced state visits, expected state visits, scheduled discharges, and the census. These are just some of the things discussed at morning meetings. Depending on where in the country you are, weather is always discussed. Whether it is snowstorms, hurricanes, tornados, earthquakes, or floods, disaster planning is reviewed often and emergency preparedness with appropriate staffing is arranged. If the president is in town, special preparations are made for him, depending on the route that he takes to visit certain events. In the event of any type of emergency or disaster, administrators, doctors, nurses, and health care team members know exactly what their roles are in the disaster preparedness plans for their particular organization. The nurse in charge has to be constantly assessing and reassessing, prioritizing, delegating, and sometimes actually doing the work itself, depending on the situation.

Nurse managers have twenty-four-hour responsibility for their units, and they make rounds with the doctors. They are involved with all patients on the unit. They monitor the patients' progress or lack of it, and the doctors give orders accordingly. The attending doctors, resident doctors, supervisors, and nurse practitioners all discuss plans for the day.

Depending on the shift nurses work, they have to deal with visitors and families and their concerns. The nurses have to always have a kind and caring attitude toward patients, visitors, and families. Understanding their pain and trying to put yourself in their position allows you to empathize and reassure the patients and their families. Often the nurse sees the worst side of the families, visitors, and patients. It seems when people are ill, their defenses are down and they just say what's on their minds without filtering. Throughout the shifts, day or night, families call to inquire about their loved ones. It is not always convenient for nurses to come to the phone or answer the phone that they are carrying, because most times they are down the hall administering medications, changing dressings, testing blood sugars, assessing the patients, and trying to stay focused on what has to be done. All this has to be accomplished in a timely manner. Many times families do not understand this.

However, when nurses speak with the family, they try to reassure them that they are just trying to give their loved one the very best care. It's not always possible to speak with them when they call. It could be that a code is in progress.

The nurse has to be careful about what s/he discusses on the phone with relatives. Again, due to HIPAA regulations and guidelines, the nurse is not able to discuss the patient's medical condition with anyone except the patient and the next of kin, recorded on the face sheet, that the patient has assigned as the health care proxy. In many instances, you are unable to tell who you are speaking to during a telephone conversation. Many institutions use a code system that callers can repeat to the nurse in order for the next of kin to gain information from the nurse.

Nurse managers follow up on issues/concerns of the patients and doctors' orders. S/he has her/his own morning meetings with the staff. The director of each service has the day's schedule of surgeries, special procedures, patient complaints, falls, disciplinary actions, staffing, and sometimes interviews with new hires. Staffing is extremely important in providing patients with the best care. The nurse manager has to staff a floor first according to the census and the acuity of the patients' needs. Then s/he has to consider the budget. S/he has to use overtime sparingly and use agency nurses who have completed orientation at the facility when necessary.

The nurse manager has to know the number of patients in isolation on the floor, and what they are being isolated for, and approximately when they will be off isolation according to the treatment required. The infection control doctor usually takes the patients off isolation when treatment is completed and after three negative cultures are obtained. However, this decision is made is in accordance with the policies and procedures of the institution where you work. Some of these issues are addressed depending on whether the setting is acute or skilled care. Managers have to know the number of decubitus ulcers (bedsores) on the floor, the number of diabetics, those on elopement precautions, those on fall precautions, those on psychotropic medications, those on dialysis with grafts or fistulas, those with current psychiatric issues, and those with Foley catheters and drains of any kind. They need to know the patients with tracheostomies, gastrostomy tubes, urostomy tubes, and colostomies. The manager constantly reinforces infection control practices according to the policy and procedures manual.

The nurse manager has to approve vacations after consulting with the assistant director of nursing and, in some cases, with the director of nursing. She does performance reviews and appraisals, and, in some cases, s/he sits in on interviews with the human resources department for hiring and for dismissal of employees. S/he attends all codes, and after each code s/he reviews the performance of the nurses and recommends improvements as appropriate.

The nurse manager attends utilization review meetings, care plan meetings, and most in-service education meetings. In nursing homes, one of the nurse manager's main responsibilities is to review all new admissions. This review includes their diagnosis, medications, all doctor's orders, allergies, diets, correct spelling on name bands, and follow-up appointments with the MDs at the hospital. The manager must identify those patients who are on fall precautions, elopement precautions, long-term antibiotics with peripherally inserted central catheter (PICC) lines and seizure precautions; those receiving physical therapy; and those who are unstable diabetics. These are just some of the things the nurse manager must know about each patient.

Sometimes in the morning meetings in a skilled care nursing facility, the administrator, the medical director, the director of nursing, and all department heads are present. Falls are discussed, and the entire team participates in recommending various methods to prevent such falls from occurring again. At that time, the incident report is signed by the team, which includes the medical director. In some nursing homes, the manager goes into patient care details, such as those on the ventilator with complications, those whose condition is deteriorating, and those with decubitus ulcers that are not healing.

After the meeting, the medical director will go and see patients who need immediate attention if their own physician is not in the house. Nurse managers monitor decubitus ulcers—patients who came in from the hospital with the ulcers and those patients who develop the ulcers in-house. If there is an infection control nurse, s/he monitors all new admissions to see those patients that are admitted with infection, those admitted with antibiotics coming from the hospital, and those who had to be placed on antibiotics at the time of admission. They monitor nosocomial infections, and those with a past history of tuberculosis (TB), methicillin-resistant staphylococcus aureus (MRSA), and many other infectious diseases. They are constantly trying to improve the standard of care by reducing infections in hospitals and nursing facilities. If there is infection, controlling it with isolation techniques reduces the risk of spreading the disease. The most important way of controlling the spread of disease is through good hand-washing techniques. This is emphasized with staff education, patient education, and visitor education. Hand sanitizers are placed in strategic locations, making them easy and convenient for use by visitors and health-care members. The sanitizers are all alcohol based to kill and prevent the spread of germs if you cannot wash your hands right away. The nurse managers make rounds with the wound care doctors and monitor the ulcers. They debride them as necessary and change treatment and medications. Detailed progress notes are kept on these patients. Infection control is critical with these ulcers, and the entire nursing staff practices good hand-washing techniques to prevent the spread of infection.

In addition, the nurse manager is responsible for doing minimum data status (MDS) and chart review. This is a state requirement in nursing homes. The federal government requires all patients who are admitted to skilled care facilities to have the following assessments: the admission assessment, the quarterly review assessment, the annual review assessment, significant change in status assessment, significant correction to prior quarterly assessment, and a whole lot more. These assessments are used to determine the financial support that the nursing home receives from the state. Having twenty-four-hour responsibility for the unit, the nurse manager is responsible for everything that takes place on the floor. Again, staffing is of the utmost importance in providing excellent nursing care according to the census and acuity.

Another one of their main functions is to check the orders carefully. They make sure that each patient receives the medication that the doctor ordered. They also have to ensure that the nurse administers the medication as ordered, and then sign the medication sheet or computer log, depending on the system used by the facility. There have been instances when a medication is not available. If the nurse signs that s/he has administered the medication, this constitutes a medication error. The manager has to discipline that nurse. The nurse has to complete a medication error form according to the policies and procedures of the institution, and the doctor has to be notified. Disciplinary action is taken by the director of nursing, and at that time the nurse can bring with her/him a representative to answer charges if the facility is unionized. A medication error can lead to termination of the nurse.

When making rounds, nurse managers have to ensure that the nurses' computers are not left open, so visitors cannot look at a patient's confidential information, or if they are using a medication book, the book has to be closed or covered. Patient information has to be protected at all times. Managers also have to check the wastepaper basket located on the side of the medication cart, and in the mediation room, they have to check for empty packages and vials with patient information. Leaving these items out is a HIPAA violation.

Patient care is a vital part of the nurse's responsibility. They have to make sure that the CNAs or PCAs give the patients a bath, oral care, and good skin care. Those patients who are unable to make their needs known have to receive complete care and be repositioned in bed every two hours. If patients are receiving tube feeding, the nursing assistants should not lower the head of the bed to a flat position. They must call the nurse to turn off the tube feeding machine first. Even after this is done, the patient should not be lying flat; this prevents aspiration of the feed from the stomach to the lungs. Too often, nursing home patients are admitted with aspiration pneumonia. After care is given, the patient must be again repositioned with the head of the bed elevated to at least a forty-five-degree angle. If a patient was instructed to take medications, but the nurse did not stay to see her/him swallow the pills, the managers on their rounds check for medication left on the bedside table. They monitor and write reports of incidents of pills found on the floor and in the patient's bed. Nurses have to be very careful in all they do because the patients' lives depend on the care that they receive.

Change of Shift Report

The report of a patient facilitates the continuation of care from one shift to the next. Nurses coming on duty should be on time. Coming fifteen minutes early is a good and professional practice, and your coworkers will be grateful for it. At the time of the report, ideally there should be no disturbances; only emergencies such as a code, a sudden change in condition, or a fall with injury should need immediate attention. The reason you must give your undivided attention at the time of the report is that you need to understand what happened on the previous shift with the patient so that you can follow through with what the day or night shift did or did not get to do on their tour.

One situation might that be a doctor has ordered a patient be put on telemetry, but two or three of the telemetry machines are out of order, and the technician will be there soon, so they are using extra telemetry boxes from another department. If a patient's condition changed, s/he should be transferred to the ICU and the physician on call should be notified. It might be that the result of the hemoglobin and hematocrit (H&H) is below a certain range, so a patient is to receive two units of packed red blood cells. As soon as you hear that, you should be thinking, *Was the blood drawn for type and cross match?; Is there consent on the chart for blood transfusion? Does the patient have IV access? What kind of veins does this patient have?"* The patient might have a line, but it is a small needle. Blood cannot go through such a tiny needle. It might be that the doctor ordered no intervention, even if the H&H is low, because the patient is a do not resuscitate (DNR) and has chronic anemia secondary to cancer. In a nursing home, the physician might write the order not to send this patient to the hospital for transfusions, but to just keep the patient comfortable with oxygen. If this is the case, the nurse must check that the DNR is current and signed by the doctor and family.

On the other hand, it could be that a patient's vancomycin level is high, and depending on the results of blood drawn earlier from the patient, the doctor wants the medication held. It could be that a patient should be discharged to another facility by a certain time and their transport does not show up. You have to call the facility because the patient already has been discharged.

It may be that it is 6 p.m., and the evening medication has not been given.

You notify the doctor again, the director of nursing, and the social worker if you are in a nursing facility. Later the patient is back in his bed dozing, and now he refuses his pills. He is told that he has been discharged, and we are still waiting for transport. The patient is alert and oriented. He has no family here in the United States, and he says even if the transport comes for him, he is not going to that facility. In such a case, the doctor has to give orders to continue treatment and medications until the morning, when the director of social service and the director of nursing can sort things out.

The nurse follows through again by notifying the physician, the director of nursing, and the social worker who made the arrangements with the other facility. The administrator also is notified at this time. The patient still needs to eat and get his medication because, even though he has been discharged, he is still considered to be a patient in the facility until he leaves the building. Proper, concise documentation would have to be made of these events, and the follow-through on this discharge would take place in the morning when all the interdisciplinary teams are present. The patient would have to be included in the census at midnight.

Another issue to follow up on could be that after a long and painful decision, the family of an ICU patient decided to make him a DNR and remove life support. This occurred after they had a meeting with the physician, the ethics committee, the head nurse, and the nurse caring for the patient. They asked to have life support removed at a designated time when some more family members from out of town would be present. The evening charge nurse was not given that report, and the physician covering had no knowledge of the decision made on the day tour. The patient was not extubated. The family was furious because the day nurse did not report the events of the day to the evening nurse, and the day nurse's notes were not concise and specific about the time the extubation should take place. The doctor's notes read, "Patient could be extubated today." The patient was extubated the next day, but not all his children were present due to work schedules and other issues. Needless to say, the family was upset, and it gave them a negative feeling toward the hospital in general. If a survey were sent to that family, the outcome would not be good.

It could be that there were two deaths in the nursing home that day, and the bodies had not been picked up as of 4 p.m. One had died late morning, and the other at the end of shift. Neither doctor had come in to sign the death certificate. The funeral homes refused to take the bodies without a death certificate signed by the doctor. When a nurse or nursing supervisor gets such a report, s/he must act immediately. S/he has to call the doctors and the funeral home as often as necessary. Once the doctor is in the house, the nurse has to call the funeral home and tell them that the death certificate is signed. S/he should remind them that the nursing home has no morgue. There is only a room with a fan, and one body is still on the floor. The nurse has to do all that s/he can to get the bodies out, even if s/ he has to ask family members to help by calling the doctor and funeral home to speed up the process. This does not occur in hospitals, because hospitals have morgues and there always are doctors in hospitals.

Part of the report could be that a culture and sensitivity (C&S) from a wound in a patient in a semiprivate room came back from the laboratory positive for MRSA. They got the results just before report began, and no one had been notified. The other patient in the room does not have MRSA. The doctor has to be notified immediately. The patient has to be told that due to medical necessity, he will be placed in an isolation room. The patient must be reassured that this is for their benefit and for the safety of the other patient as well, to prevent the spread of infection. The patient's family has to be notified about the room change, and communications must be clearly documented in the chart. After report is completed, this should be one of the first things on the agenda for the next shift so as not to put the other patient at risk. After the doctor, the next of kin, and the patient have been informed, isolation procedures have to be taken; signs must be placed on the door, and the report has to be given to the nurses and nursing assistants who will be caring for that patient. Appropriate medications must be ordered and started. Isolation can be discontinued when treatment is completed, and when three consecutive negative cultures have been taken forty-eight hours after completion of treatment for MRSA. All outbreaks of communicable diseases in hospitals and nursing facilities must be reported to the public health department.

The scenarios described above are just some of the things that would be passed on during report from shift to shift.

Sometimes during the report, a code is called. If this happens in a skilled care facility (nursing home), the nurse should know if the patient has a DNR order. This information can be found in the front of the chart. The nurse should be aware of all the patients on her/his floor who are DNRs, and as soon as a code is called, s/ he has to check the status on the chart. I have seen and heard of family members signing a DNR, but when the patient's condition deteriorated and the patient went into cardiac or respiratory arrest, the next of kin or family member with power of attorney said, "I don't want my mother to be a DNR. I want everything done for my mother." At this point, the nurse had to comply with the family's request to be sure and legally safe. Always call 911 when there is no indication on the form what the family wants done. If there is no DNR in the chart, then CPR must be initiated until 911 arrives. The time of the arrest if it was witnessed, or the time when the patient was found to be unresponsive must be documented.

A Day in the Life of a Nurse

Once a nurse is off of orientation and s/he is on her/his own, s/he takes report from the shift going off duty and counts the narcotics to make sure the count is correct. Now many hospitals use a system in which narcotics are secured in a machine that is programmed by a code. Both shifts have to check narcotics together before the keys or the code for the computerized narcotic dispenser are handed over, and each narcotic count has to be correct before the nurses can sign off. On the 3-to-11 tour, after making rounds and following up on issues from day tour, s/he has to deal with admissions, dietary requirements, the families, falls, 911 emergencies, and deaths. Some days can be overwhelming, to say the least.

For example, you could get an admission who is in poor condition from a hospital. Once the patient is settled in bed and you review the orders, you realize that this patient probably has pneumonia because of the rhonchi in her lungs, fever, coughing, and poor oxygen saturation (O2Sat). You notify the physician and obtain orders for stat X-ray and antibiotics. The order is then faxed to the pharmacy. The doctor comes in an hour later, and the patient has to be coded, 911 is called, and after half an hour of continuous CPR, the patient is pronounced dead by the doctor.

As the nursing supervisor in charge, you get a call to evaluate a patient who is confused and has fallen out of her wheelchair. After you've assessed the patient on the floor to evaluate for fractures, the patient is lifted off the floor and placed in bed. The patient suffered head and facial lacerations, and emergency treatment is given. Then the patient has to be transferred to the hospital. You clean the areas of laceration and apply cold compresses while the patient is waiting to be transferred to the hospital. Aside from the doctor, the family has to be notified, and the transfer papers are written and copied and given to the emergency medical technicians (EMTs). If the patient is a DNR, those papers have to copied and sent with the transfer papers. Before the patient leaves, she must be checked to see if s/he has a wristband with the correct spelling of her name. An incident report has to be written. Just as you are writing it, you get a call from another floor that there is a new admission. As soon as the supervisor and the nurse on that floor walk into the patient's room, she takes her last breath. This patient is a DNR. The doctor has to be notified. He in turn notifies the family. The floor nurse and the nursing assistant prepare the body appropriately as per protocol of the institution, and the patient is placed in a temporary holding area until the funeral home picks up the body, unless the family requests to see the body before leaving the floor. The doctor has signed the death certificate. Everything has to be thoroughly documented, and when the family calls, the nurse has to be prepared to give condolences on behalf of the staff and to comfort them as best as s/he can. The person from the funeral home signs the appropriate forms required by the facility, and this has to be entered into a log that is kept in the nursing office.

This is not an everyday event, but admissions are. Transferring patients back and forth to the hospital regularly occurs in a nursing facility. The following day the nurse manager has to check and make sure that all documentation is appropriate and correct. The charts of the patients who are transferred to the hospital and those who expire are then sent to medical records after a complete audit of the chart is done. All of these series of occurrences just mentioned have happened on one shift, although this is not an everyday event. However, most times the units are very busy.

Things that we used to do in the seventies are now in some cases obsolete. We are now in the new age of technology; computers are our means of caring for our patients in terms of documenting, picking up doctor's orders, and scanning the patients' name bands before medication administration. You now are able to view the patient's history and physical diagnosis, allergies and all the demographics right on the computer.

Stress and apprehension are evident in dealing with the very sick patients. They depend on the nurse for encouragement and emotional support. There are always concerned relatives with questions, unannounced state surveyors in the building, and nurses running behind on their schedules for medication and treatments. Many times nurses do not even have a chance to eat because there is so much going on.

There are times when you feel like no one can see all that you do. Instead, you are constantly reminded that God sees your heart, and he sees what you do to help the patients overcomes their illness. There are times when your supervisor sees only what you did wrong or failed to do; yet each day you come to work and it warms your heart when you see your patients recover from surgery, or whatever their illness was, and they come to say good-bye to you; or when you see them survive a code in the ICU and be transferred to the step-down unit. In a nursing home, when they recover and are discharged to go home with family, they come to the desk with a big smile to tell you they are going home, and you can hear the expressions of appreciation in their voices. Sometimes it brings tears to your eyes.

On the other hand, there are times when everything is done to save patients, yet they die because of their diagnosis and the advanced stage of their illness. You feel sad, and each death takes a toll. Each death is like the first you have experienced. It still feels the same each time, because a human life is lost. Later when the family calls to say thank you for the wonderful care you gave to their mother or father, it eases the pain knowing that they appreciated all that you did. Sometimes you are off for a few days, and when you return to work, the patients tell you how much they've missed you. It makes you feel special and tells you that you are needed and appreciated, and that God put you in this position to help your fellow man.

Admission Process

The admission process is extremely important when residents are admitted from the acute care hospital setting to the nursing home. One of the first things that happen when the patient arrives is that the family comes to the nursing station wanting to speak with the doctor. They often have problems with the transition from the acute care hospital to the nursing home. Nursing homes do not have doctors on the premises twenty-four hours a day, , although they can be reached readily. The family sometimes feels that you should stop what you are doing to answer all of their questions immediately. Because this is not always possible given the nurse/patient ratio in the nursing home, the families often get upset. The nurse/patient ratio in the nursing home is usually twenty-five to thirty patients per nurse. This kind of ratio is new to the family and patients, and it is sometimes a problem for them. In the hospital, the nurses have six to eight patients maximum. In the ICU, the ratio is one nurse to two or maybe three patients. In spite of the nurse's workload, s/he has to demonstrate patience and understanding with the family. With the excellent customer service training that nurses receive in orientation, you could turn things around by the way you speak and interact with the patient and family members. Some families are just concerned, while others are angry for whatever their reasons are.

Customer service is important in every organization, and many times you will be expected to be the representative for the facility. It is important to treat everyone with respect and dignity, going out of your way to offer help and speaking in a soft voice. Remember, the patients and their families come first. You are there to help them with their fears and anxieties in coping with their illness. Dressing appropriately in your uniform with your name tag visible and always being polite can help to bridge this gap. Remember that first impressions count and last. You are the frontline representative of your hospital or nursing facility. It is not the administrator or the director of nursing that the visitors and patients see on admission and on a regular basis. It is the nurse and the nursing assistant that they meet as they enter the floor in the facility. It is you who could determine if the family wants their relative to stay in the facility. If they get the feeling from you that you understand them and are willing to listen to and assist them, then they will begin to trust you, thereby allaying their fears.

Regardless of how you feel or what personal problems you are dealing with, once you come through those doors to work, put on a smile and concentrate on the task at hand. Conduct yourself in a professional manner at all times. In doing so, you will build trust and respect among the patients and your peers. You give the patient's family a sense of comfort and satisfaction when you make them feel safe and important. This will help them build trust in the nurses and the CNAs, and it will increase patient satisfaction, reducing complaints and negative outcomes.

Before a patient is admitted to a long-term care facility, there has to be a meeting with the admissions office. Liaisons from the facility go to various hospitals and tell them about the various services their facilities offer. They get to know the doctors, who in turn will send their patients to a rehab facility that they feel will be suited and beneficial for that patient. The doctor has to recommend that the patient requires skilled rehabilitation services on a daily basis and establish that this service can be provided only on an in-patient basis. Medicare requires fourteen-day, thirty-day- and sixty-day recertification for continuation of these services. The admissions office in the skilled nursing facility (SNF) checks the patient's insurance and the number of days left for rehab services. The family signs financial documents and legal agreements regarding their responsibilities. In most cases, a family member and/or next of kin sign forms authorizing treatment of the patient by the attending physician.

The attending physician in turn requests consultations with members of other disciplines that might be needed, such as dentistry, podiatry, laboratory, X-ray, audiology, ophthalmology, and wound care. He coordinates the care of the patient with the nursing director. The medical director oversees all the doctors in the facility and monitors the care that all patients receive by making rounds and reviewing charts.

Once the admission agreement has been signed and the nursing home liaisons have obtained all the necessary information about the patient, then the nursing home accepts the patient. The hospital then transfers the patient via ambulance or ambulate to the designated nursing home. Two EMTs usually accompany the patient from the hospital bed to the nursing home, where they transfer the patient from the stretcher to the bed. In most cases, the nurse is aware that an admission is expected. However, when the admission arrives, the bed might not be available due to various circumstances, such as a late discharge or because the bed has not yet been cleaned. Sometimes, the previous resident's belongs are still in the closet. Luckily, this is not the case most times. If this does happen, housekeeping is notified immediately, and the clothes are removed and the closet is cleaned.

The nurse welcomes the patient and family, and performs a quick assessment of the patient before the EMTs transfer the resident into the bed. This is very important because the patient might have a very high fever, be in respiratory distress, or have very high or very low blood pressure. If there is a problem, the doctor needs to be notified and the patient must be taken back to the hospital. It is best for this assessment to take place before the sheet of acceptance from the hospital is signed because once the EMTs leave you may find that the patient needs to go back to the hospital. If that happens, you have to do an admission, and then a discharge back to the hospital. That requires a lot of unnecessary time.

When being transferred from the hospital, the patient usually brings a discharge summary that contains the patient's history and physical examination results, and it usually lists the patient's chief complaint upon admission to the hospital. The history covers the patient's illness, past medical and surgical history, maybe some social history, and information about medical procedures and tests that were done in the hospital. The list contains information about allergies, immunizations, TB status, and whether or not the patient is on isolation and why s/he that must be continued in the nursing home. Sometimes the sheet also will show the medications that the patient took prior to this hospitalization.

The discharge summary usually shows the date that the patient was admitted to the hospital and the discharge date. Most important is the discharge diagnosis, including the primary diagnosis and secondary diagnosis, such as coronary artery disease, or coronary artery bypass graft (CABG) with the date the surgery was performed. This patient might still have staples in his or chest that must be removed on a certain date by the surgeon. The nurse makes a note for the secretary to schedule follow-up appointments for the patient.

Secondary diagnoses may be seizure disorder, diabetes mellitus type II, hypertension, and sacral decubitus. Sometimes the sacral decubitus ulcer is not staged at the time of admission from the hospital. The nurse measures the height, width, and depth of the ulcer and stages it according to policy for when the wound care doctor sees the patient the next day. The nurse also photographs the decubitus ulcer for the records. When the photograph is taken, the patient's name, medical record number, the location of the wound, and the date the picture was taken should be clearly identified and labeled on the photograph. Many hospitals today have cameras specifically for this use. The pictures tell you exactly the stage of the wound and the condition of the wound at the time of admission. Careful documentation of ulcers is important because many times the families or the transferring hospitals will say that the patient did not leave their care with a wound in that state. The nursing facility will have to take the blame if no pictures or accurate documentation have been made by the nurse.

Patients are admitted with many illnesses, such as multiple myeloma, end-stage renal disease, Alzheimer's disease, S/P, myocardial infarction (heart attack), strokes, and many other medical problems. Once the patient is settled in bed, a full patient assessment is done by the registered nurse. The attending physician has to approve all medications, which then must be faxed to the pharmacy. The patient receives a tray with the appropriate diet and is later given a bath by the CNA. Some nursing home records are computer based; after all the medications have been reviewed by the physician on the telephone and read back to make sure that there are no errors, the medication orders are then entered into the computer and submitted to the pharmacy.

The pharmacist often calls for clarification if an order is entered incorrectly or the dose of a medication is wrong. In that case, the doctor is then called, the error is corrected, and the pharmacist is informed. If the nursing home uses a computer, then the original order is automatically discontinued. This procedure is quite different from that in the hospital because the hospital has its own pharmacy and pharmacist on the premises twenty-four hours a day. Doctors are always present—not necessarily the attending physician, but the physician that covers the emergency room, the ICUs, and the special care units, and the resident doctors who deal with critical life-and-death situations. There is always a doctor to write orders and take care of emergencies on the spot.

In some instances, hospitals and nursing homes have patients with the same last name on the same unit. This is immediately identified and addressed with red name alert stickers. Various institutions use different methods to deal with this issue, but the important thing is to make sure that a system is in place to prevent medical and medication errors.

In discharging the patient from the acute care hospital, the doctor makes clear the primary diagnosis. In the case of hip surgery, there are certain hip precautions that have to be adhered to, depending on how the surgery was done. In some cases, the doctors do an open reduction and internal fixation. Those residents have to have an abduction pillow between their legs at all times. Even when they are turning in bed, the pillow stays between their legs. Those with fractured hips usually have a dressing, but sometimes the doctor does not want it changed. This must be noted on your nurse's notes. He himself will come in the next day to change it. These patients are not weighed on admission. Weighing the patient could put the patient at risk for hip dislocation. Strict hip precautions must be adhered to. The patient is first seen by the physical therapist the next day and evaluated. The therapist decides what scale should be used to weigh the patient after consulting with the doctor.

Other patients come from the hospital who are on long-term antibiotic for diseases such as osteomyelitis (infection in the bone), or for an infectious disease of the colon called Clostridium difficile (Cdiff). This is an infectious disease of the colon that causes loose, foul-smelling stools. Patients with this diagnosis are put on isolation immediately to prevent the spread of infection. All this is done in accordance with the infection control policies of the institution. Those on isolation should have their own blood pressure machine and thermometer in their rooms. As with all infectious diseases, treatment would entail setting up an isolation room for the patient after explaining to the patient and family the importance of preventing the spread of infection and reinforcing good hand-washing techniques. Sometimes wearing gowns and masks is required.

There are patients who come to the nursing home who need to wear a BIPAP machine at night because of sleep apnea. This requirement should be included on the transfer notes from the hospital. The machine and the settings of the machine should be ordered before the time of transfer to be sure that they get to the nursing home before the patient arrives. The hospital orders the BIPAP machine from its preferred vendor. The settings are programmed as ordered by the physician before it is brought to the nursing home. All the nurse has to do is to explain the procedure to the patient and apply the mask at bedtime. Some patients have used it in the hospital or at home, while others have not. Some patients become very apprehensive, and the nurse has to explain how the machine works. Sometimes the patient is confused and afraid of the BIPAP machine. As soon as the nurse puts it on, he or she takes it off. If this is the case, the doctor and the family should be notified. The nurse should make frequent rounds and reassess the patient to see if he or she needs it by doing an oxygen saturation assessment with and without the machine. If the doctor decides that the patient needs it, the nurse has to make frequent rounds and replace the BIPAP each time that the patient takes it off. The family has to be notified, and it has to be documented in the charts.

If the patient is in a semiprivate room and is alert and oriented, s/he should be introduced to the roommate, depending on the roommate's cognitive status. Before leaving the room, the nurse or CNA should always make sure that the call light, the light switch, and the bedside table are within reach of the patient. Fresh water and tissue should be on the table. During the admission interview, the nurse should find out the last time the patient had a bowel movement. If it has been at least three days, the doctors should be informed, and maybe he will order milk of magnesia or other laxatives along with a stool softener at bedtime.

In summary, the new admission should have a nursing assessment done from head to toe. The oral cavity, face, chest, abdomen, perineal area, and extremities should be assessed. Contractures and locations of the contractures; open lesions; wrist/foot drop; height; weight, prostheses such as glasses, hearing aids, artificial limbs, and pacemakers; eating habits and diet; gastrostomy tubes; bowel and bladder history; sleep habits; and language spoken must be included. The patient's smoking history should be reviewed. This is very important for prevention of fires. All cigarettes and lighters should be removed from the patient's possession on admission. Most hospitals and nursing homes have a no smoking policy. The nursing homes that don't will have the patients smoke in a designated outside area on the first floor with a staff member present.

Social history such as hobbies; previous occupation; religion; marital status; activities of daily living (ADL) skills, such as bathing, dressing and transferring; and the ability to understand verbal and written instructions must be assessed. Skin condition should be thoroughly checked because the hospital does not always indicate all the marks, scars, sores, pressure ulcers, and ecchymotic areas that are present on the patient's skin at the time of discharge. Oral assessment should include teeth, gums, missing teeth, dentures —upper, lower, and partial—difficulty chewing and swallowing, and the presence of mouth pain. Any allergies to medication should be indicated on the chart and on the patient's name bands. Each admission should be given a new band with the name spelled correctly. The wristband should indicate allergies, diabetes, pacemakers, and dialysis, if applicable.

The nurse's notes should be very detailed. The doctor's notes deal mostly with the date of admission, admitting diagnosis, final diagnosis when the patient left the hospital, a brief history and essential findings during the course of the stay in the hospital, and a final disposition of discharge. The nurse's notes are much more detailed. They include the following: date and time of admission, resident's name, room number, name of hospital admitted from, hospital admission date, hospital discharge date, and the hospital discharge diagnosis. They check for significant findings on the following: skin; mental status; abdomen; heart and lungs; pelvic, genital, and rectal areas; extremities; breasts; drug regimen and treatment; and care plan. The nurses also are responsible for incident reports or occurrence reports, which include the patient's name, room number, date and time of the occurrence, exact location of the occurrence, description of the occurrence by the patient (if the patient is able to give one),staff account of the occurrence, and the immediate action that was taken. Occurrence reports are vital for the institution and the state. On many state visits, they ask to see different incident reports, both recent and from a couple years previous.

The nursing evaluation/assessment includes vital signs; physical and mental status; patient's diagnosis; name of the physician notified, date and time; name of next of kin that was notified, date and time; relationship to the resident; and the person who writes the occurrence notes, date and time. The name of the supervisor on duty, the date and time s/he was notified, X-rays and other tests ordered, whether or not the patient was sent to the hospital, and the date and time of the examination also should be included. It is important to mark the injured part of the body in the chart. It also is important to note if the patient is on psychotropic medications, the name of the medication, the dosage, and the last time a dose was administered prior to the incident/accident.

In certain long-term care hospitals, a patient who has a DNR order who has expired in the absence of a physician may be pronounced dead by the qualified registered nurse if the patient's physician is not in the hospital and the patient's death was anticipated with orders in the medical records for do not resuscitate. In order to do this, the qualified nursing supervisor will independently assess the patient and document in the medical records cessation of cardiopulmonary function to include the following:

a) Lack of response to stimuli

b) Absence of spontaneous respiration for a minimum of sixty seconds

c) Absence of pulse detected by listening with a stethoscope to the chest for a minimum of sixty seconds

d) Absence of blood pressure

e) Lack of pupillary response

The nursing supervisor will document the clinical findings and will document the date and time of the pronouncement of death. The doctor will come in and verify the findings. The nursing supervisor is able to do this in accordance with the policies and procedures of institutions in some states.

Pain assessment and evaluation are done by the nurse when the patient comes from the hospital. Sometimes the patient is in great pain and pain medication has been ordered for the patient but it is yet to be ordered from the admitting institution's pharmacy. In those instances, the nursing supervisor uses medication from the emergency medication kept double-locked in the nursing office as required by the state and the institution. The drug is obtained for the patient for the relief of pain, and a dose is ordered from the pharmacy for replacement in the emergency medication kit. Once the medication has been given, the nurse has to note the time given, when it took effect, and how much of the pain was relieved on a scale of 1 to 10. Different institutions use different types of evaluation techniques to evaluate pain. The comfort level with regard to pain is one of the most important things in healing and recovery. If a medication is not effective, the physician is notified and the dosage is modified or the medication is changed. The nurses help the doctors in more ways than you can imagine. They are the ones with the patient eight to twelve hours a day, and they see a lot during that time. They keep the physician informed so he can make appropriate changes in the care of the patient.

Postoperatively, when the patient is awakening from anesthesia, the pain can be very intense. The sounds that patients utter can be heart-wrenching. This is often seen in recovery rooms now called the post-anesthesia care unit. On the floors of nursing homes, when patients feel pain, it is very important to give them their pain medication without delay so that they can feel comfortable. Patients should be educated that they are not to wait until the last minute when the pain becomes intense to ask for their medication, because at that time, the medication does not always work. Most patients know when to start asking for pain medication. Those that are confused or disoriented should be given pain medication when it is due to prevent needless suffering.

To ensure effective pain management, pain medication should be ordered on an as-needed (PRN) basis. Pain medications also should be given prior to physical therapy and certain procedures or activities that cause pain. Some examples are dressing changes, getting out of bed for very sick patients, and procedures that doctors perform at the bedside. The ultimate goal of pain management is to free the patient of pain. However, if the patient's diagnosis is terminal and the pain is intense, then the goal is to control and minimize the pain to the fullest extent possible. On admission, if a patient has a decubitus ulcer, the pain can be intense at times. It is especially important to understand this and to keep patients medicated if they are unable to make their needs known. Nurses have to be understanding and make sure that they administer pain medication when it is due or when the patient asks for it, without delay. To wait until a patient is screaming in pain is totally unacceptable.

There are some evenings when you have as many as seven or eight admissions throughout the nursing facility and the nurses are stressed. Perhaps not everything can be completed that day. However, doctors' orders including medications are always done, and the patient is always made comfortable and kept safe. The following day the admission process can be completed.

Some days you're having a fairly good evening, and when you go to administer medication to Mrs. Jones, who is on elopement precautions, she is nowhere to be found in the house. The nurse notifies the supervisor, the elopement code is called, and staff throughout the building begin the search. Luckily, Mrs. Jones is found in the basement near the cafeteria trying to get a soda from the soda machine. She is unharmed, but she is confused and does not know where she is or how she got there. Her CNA and nurse are held accountable for their patients, especially the ones on elopement precautions. Most elevators now have a code that must be entered in order to leave the floor. The doctor, the director of nursing, and the administrator are notified. However, the state does not need to be notified, because the patient did not leave the building. Appropriate documentation is done, and the staff responsible are counseled. If the patient leaves via the stairs, an alarm will sound.

There have been incidents, however, when the patient has left the institution, taken a bus, and was found many miles away. In such a case, the police, the doctor, the family, the administrator, and the director of nursing were all notified. The state was also notified, appropriate documentation was noted in the patient's chart, and the next day the state made a visit. By then, the police had found and returned the patient to the nursing home. The doctor performed a physical examination, and the registered nurse performed a full assessment. The staff was immediately in-service regarding preventative measures on elopement precautions, and the care plan was updated. The patient was given a shower and a complete assessment of the skin was done; then a tray was ordered and brought to the patient. Cognitive functions were the same as prior to elopement. The patient was confused and unable to say what had happened. The family was kept informed throughout the incident.

After each elopement, the nurses and CNAs have to be educated by the educational coordinator and the nursing supervisor. The staff must check on their patients at least every hour, especially those that are on elopement precautions, because sometimes these patients revert to their former lifestyle or habits. They think they are still working or have to be someplace at a given time. Education of the staff helps to prevent elopement, and the security bracelet should be checked daily to make sure that it is in proper working condition so that the alarm will go off once the patient exits through an exterior door to leave the building.

Once the supervisor comes on duty, s/he has to check staffing to make sure that all the staff are in the building and on their assigned units. When s/he makes rounds, s/he sees to it that the nurses have checked their emergency equipment on the floor (i.e., the suctioning machine is operational, oxygen tanks are filled and ready to be used, and the crash cart is ready). S/he makes rounds in all the rooms and finds out from the nurses any outstanding events that are happening or have happened, or others that s/he should be aware of. Usually there are two nurses on each floor, with a census of thirty to fifty patients on each unit. When the nurse goes to supper, the other nurse has to cover for her/him. If a crisis should arise, s/he can call the supervisor, who will come immediately. Based on the nurse's clinical assessment, the doctor can make changes appropriate to patient care when s/he is not present.

The CNAs on the floor are extremely important because they perform various duties for the patients: bathe them, feed them, toilet them, put them into and take them out of bed, and report any and all changes to the nurse. They have to document how the patients ate, whether or not they urinated or had a BM, or if they have observed a change in the patient's condition. They also report all complaints to the nurses. The nurses could not do their jobs without the assistance of the CNAs or PCAs. They are in effect a blessing to the nurses in the same way the nurses are to the doctors.

The night shift is somewhat different from the evenings. To start with, most of the residents are asleep. There are no visitors most of the time; however, in some states now, visiting hours are allowed twenty-four hours a day, and some visitors stay throughout the night. Nursing facilities are no longer announcing by overhead page that visiting hours are over. No patients have to go to physical therapy or have procedures done. There are no clinic appointments, no patients are out on pass with family members, and no doctors are making rounds unless there is a decline in a patient's condition. Once the nurse takes the report, counts narcotics, checks the emergency carts, and administers the night's medications and treatment, most of the time you will be auditing charts and setting up medications to be given early in the morning. You make sure that patients who are going for procedures in the hospital the next day are given nothing to eat or drink (NPO). The nurse will administer pain medications, make sure that the CNAs change the patients and reposition them as needed, and check their gastrostomy tube feedings and the rate of infusion. They make up new bags to be hung in the morning.

Special rounds are made for all new diabetic patients to make sure they are not in crisis, whether they are hypo- or hyperglycemic. Many IV antibiotics are given in the morning at 6 a.m., and glucose testing also is done at that time. For those patients who to have fasting blood work, the nurse must communicate with the patient and CNAs. They have to be made aware so that the patient does not eat before the blood is drawn. Specimens are collected early because the technicians are in the building to collect specimens and draw blood by 5 a.m. Those patients who are going to dialysis have to have an early breakfast sent up, and their medications are held until after they return from dialysis. The last tap water enema has to be given early in the morning for those going for gastrointestinal procedures. Patients who have pulled out their gastrostomy tubes have to be sent to the hospital for replacement. However, some physicians replace the gastrostomy tubes at the patient's bedside, so the nurse has to make sure that all the needed equipment is present on the floor.

Flashlights always should be available on the night tour in order to avoid turning on the overhead lights and waking the patients. However, sometimes it is necessary to turn on the lights, depending on what the nurse has to do—such as administer medications, change a dressing, give a treatment, draw blood, or restart an infiltrated IV.

There are times when a patient has to go to the hospital for a special procedure and during the procedure, the patient codes. The anesthesiologist intubates the patient, and the CPR board is placed under the patient's back for initiation of CPR. Electrocardiograph leads are then attached to the patient, and the cardiac monitor shows the rhythm that the patient is in. If the patient has a flat line, cardiac compressions are initiated. The attending doctor sees from the cardiac monitor what rhythm the patient's heart is in and orders medication accordingly. The nurse has to have a code sheet on which s/he documents the time the code was called, the drugs and the time each drug was administered, and the events that preceded the code. After the patient is stabilized, s/he is transported to the intensive care unit. The patient's attending physician and the family are informed. The ICU is notified that a patient is being transferred to the unit. Report is given at that time, and the nurse is informed whether or not the patient is on isolation. A nurse, a doctor, and a respiratory therapist accompany the patient to the unit.

Sometimes a code is witnessed by the nurse or the PCA during rounds. Immediately CPR is started, and the code team is notified. It is announced over the hospital public address system. Each institution has its own code name (Code 99, Code Blue, Code 711, Team 7000, etc.). Again, once the patient is stabilized and the code sheet is appropriately filled out, the patient is transferred to the unit and everyone is notified. Nurses in the ICU have only two or three patients to care for. It is a very different care situation than on the floor. There are lots of machines, and a lot goes on with one patient at any given time. A doctor is always present in the ICU, so their codes are almost never announced over the PA system.

Documentation is the key to understanding all that happens to the patient. Maintaining professional medical records is vital. It cannot be overemphasized how important it is to document in detail events as they occur. If this is done, the patient will receive the best care possible, lawsuits will be reduced, and positive outcomes and positive state surveys will be produced. If an action was not documented, it was not done for all intents and purposes, because there is no way to tell if it was done unless it is written in the medical records. Sometimes lawsuits occur. When you go to court, the judge is going to ask, "Where is the documentation for what you are telling me?" In most cases, the patient received the care, treatment, and medication, but these actions were not documented in the charts.

As a nurse, if you forget to sign for medication that was given, you must notify the manager for that unit immediately as you become aware of the oversight, even if you are at home or have just left the facility. Sometimes you must return to the nursing facility, but you must notify them before you can go to sleep. This is extremely important because when these patients leave the hospital and their charts go to the medical records department, the records cannot be completed unless everything has been signed for. The administrative supervisor in charge of the nursing facility has keys for the nursing office and the narcotics cabinet, and the master key for everything in the facility. If you make a mistake and take these keys home, regardless of how far away you live, you must return them to the facility immediately.

When you consider that in the nursing home you have thirty to fifty patients per floor, and half of those patients are under your care, it can become overwhelming. On the evening and night shifts, there is less staff. Yet there are still medications, treatments, dressing changes, and glucose monitoring, among other things that the nurse has to do. No one is sitting at the nursing station to answer the telephone, and families often call wanting to know about their family members when the nurse is trying to administer medications down the hall. It can be quite stressful on all tours, but especially on the night and evening tours.

Example of a Hospital Admission Note

11/09/2012, 3:15 p.m. This is a fifty-year-old male diabetic, admitted to the hospital after a chain saw he was using at work completely severed his left thumb. He was alone when it happened, and he was unable to find his thumb. He wrapped his finger and drove to the nearest hospital. When he got word to his wife and daughter, the daughter went to the location where he had been working, found the thumb, put it on ice, and returned it to the hospital. The patient had to be transferred to another hospital where there was a surgeon who could reattach his thumb. After eight hours of surgery, they were unable to attach the finger successfully due to the damaged and flailed nerve endings caused by the chain saw. This made it impossible for the surgeon to reattach the finger because it was not a clean cut. A graft was taken from two different sides of his body to graft the area of the missing thumb. At 3:00 a.m. on 11/10/2012, the post-anesthesia care unit (PACU) nurse called to give report to the floor nurse before transferring him to the floor. On arrival to 5 North, the patient appears drowsy but alert and oriented when fully awakened. V/S—BP 128/76; P 28; R 20; O2Sat 96% on room air. Patient has a dilaudid drip via a PCA pump in a peripheral vein in his right arm. This was piggybacked to his main IV line, which was 0.45 normal saline at 75 cc per hour. His lungs are clear, heart rate regular, abdomen soft. Foley catheter No. 16—30 cc in situ draining clear, amber urine. At present 300 cc urine is in his Foley bag. The skin is clean, and the left arm is bandaged and is in a sling that is elevated on an IV pole. A small area of the hand is left open. Hemovac draining from wound—small amount serosanguineous drainage noted in hemovac. Patient is complaining of pain in left hand, nausea, and itching over his body. On a pain scale of 1 to 10, the patient said his pain was a 9. The doctor on call was notified, and he ordered a bolus of dilaudid and some Benadryl. Medication was given as ordered. V/S were monitored before and after medication was administered. The BP dropped a little to 116/70; P 80; O2Sat remains the same. An hour later, BP was back to 120/68; P 84; R 17. Patient was resting comfortably in bed with his daughter dozing in a chair at the bedside. There were no complaints throughout the rest of the night, and V/S remain stable at time of report at 7 a.m. Total intake and output: IV 300 cc, Foley drain total 500 cc clear amber urine (3 a.m. to 7 a.m.). Patient remains NPO.

Signed: Jackie Forrest, RN

Nursing Home Admission

In the nursing home, the assessment of all new admissions is done by the registered nurse with the assistance of the licensed practical nurse. In accepting the patient from the hospital, the nurse has to do a complete assessment from head to toe. S/he has to make sure the patient is breathing and has vital signs within the range that the nursing home can care for. S/he has to check whether or not the patient is semi-comatose, is on oxygen, or is looking flushed. The temperature is checked with an oral thermometer. Patients with fevers over 102oF orally, difficulty breathing, hypotension with systolic blood pressure less than 80, or finger sticks over 500 mg/dl should be sent back to the hospital. However, if there is a DNR order that has been signed by the physician and next of kin, then you can admit the patient into the nursing home.

There have been instances when patients have been sent back to the hospital because of high fevers, no antibiotic therapy, and no intravenous lines to give antibiotics. These patients usually have poor veins that require skilled professionals to put in a PICC line for long-term antibiotic therapy. Some have been sent out on the same stretcher with the same EMT personnel who brought them to the nursing home. Usually two EMTs transport the patient; one is usually in charge of handling the paperwork, while the other one secures the patient on the stretcher. Registered nurses are taught to do a quick visual assessment of the patient while s/he is on the stretcher. Based on the nurse's assessment and the notification of the doctor, the decision is made whether or not to accept the patient or send her/him back to the hospital.

Once the patient is admitted into the nursing home, notifying the doctor and reviewing the medications with him are of paramount importance. In some instances, the physician who cared for the patient during the hospital stay is the same doctor who continues to care for the patient in the nursing home. This is very good for the patient in terms of continuity of care because the doctor knows the patient and may already have a rapport with the family. He is the one who writes the discharge orders and medication orders from the hospital to the nursing home. However, it is the policy of the institution that you still have to call the doctor and review with him each individual medication.

Sometimes when you check the patient on admission, you find that what looks like a simple dressing is really a drain under a dressing. Nowhere in the transfer orders is there any notation about the drain. You have to call the hospital and speak with the nurse who cared for that patient and then call the doctor again and get orders from him. The nurse needs to ask questions such as, When was the drain put in? Was it after a surgical procedure? When was it done? Is it to be connected to a drainage bag? How often should it be drained? And the list goes on. The site has to be checked for infection, and the dressing has to be changed as ordered unless there is a specific order not to change the dressing until the doctor sees the patient.

Example of a Nursing Home Admission Note

11/29/2012, 4:15 p.m. Patient is an eighty-five-year-old East Indian female who lives with her grandson and his wife. The patient is confused and speaks very little English. She was admitted to St. Mary's Skilled Care Facility with a diagnosis of fractured right femur, dementia, dehydration, and coronary disease. Grandson Michael states that his grandmother has progressively gotten more confused with frequent falls, and in the last month she has been incontinent of bowel and bladder. She had not seen a doctor for over a year until five days ago, when she was admitted to the hospital for a fractured right femur. On examination, the patient is alert but confused and appears to be afraid of strangers. The grandson's wife assisted the RN with her examination and assessment of the patient. The skin is warm and dry. She has poor skin turgor—appears dehydrated and malnourished. Lungs are clear bilaterally. Heart rate regular 84/minute; BP 110/65; respiration 24; O2Sat 94% on room air. The abdomen is soft and non-distended. The patient had a BM prior to discharge from the hospital. The genital area is clean. The skin on the back and sacral area is intact. Femoral and pedal pulses are present. Both feet are warm to the touch. The dressing on the right femur was removed to examine the surgical site. The dressing was replaced with a sterile dressing. No signs or symptoms of infection were noted. Staples are intact. The patient has an appointment to see the surgeon in two weeks. Weight is 105 pounds with the chair scale. Height is five feet. A partial bed-bath was given. The patient was made comfortable in bed. Demonstrated to family member and patient how to use the call light. The bedside table is within the patient's reach. The family explained same to the patient. Unable to assess if the patient understands. Orders from hospital were reviewed and confirmed with the attending physician. Medication orders were then faxed to the pharmacy. The patient was placed on a low-sodium, chopped diet. There are orders for physical therapy (PT) and occupational therapy (OT) evaluation and treatment. This is a short-term admission, and the plan is for the patient to return home after rehab. At present, the patient is attempting to get out of bed. The family has been asked to stay with the patient until she becomes familiar with her surroundings and staff members. The bed was placed in the low position. Asked family member to ask the patient if she has pain in her right leg. The patient told her family that she did not. Transfer notes indicate that she was medicated for pain just before leaving the hospital. Asked family member to write down in her native language with the English translation words such as "pain in leg"; "going to therapy"; "we want to get you out of bed"; "are you comfortable?"; "it's time to eat"; "it's time to take a bed-bath." The family was very cooperative. The list was placed above the bed-head for all disciplines to see if family is not present.

Signed June Mullings, RN

Sick Calls: When Nurses Call in Sick

When nurses call in sick, it disrupts the entire scheduling in the hospital or nursing home. Depending on the institution's policy, you may be able to call a nurse from an agency with which you have a contract, or you can call nurses who are on their scheduled day off. But you must replace the nurse or the nurse's aide in order to give good nursing care. Some facilities have a mandatory staffing requirement; that is, there has to be certain ratios of patients to nurses and CNAs to patients. In some states, if this rule is violated, you can be penalized and placed on moratorium. Replacing nurses who work in specialized care areas is quite difficult because they have to be knowledgeable of that specific area of nursing. The ICUs, telemetry units, and transplant units in many hospitals are closed. That is, if nurses call in sick, then they rearrange the schedule and replace themselves because floating a floor nurse into these units would be too stressful for the nurse.

Nurses should take a lunch break and two other breaks throughout the day if they are working a twelve-hour day. When the nurses do not eat and get time to have five minutes for themselves, they can become irritable and less understanding. It is very important for nurses to get off the unit to "de-stress," clear their minds, refresh, eat, and relax. Sometimes just walking outside for a few minutes, taking in the fresh air, can revitalize the nurse and increase her/his energy and performance. Nurses have to work together; if the unit is extremely busy, all the nurses on the unit have to look out for each other. They need to make a point of taking care of each other so that they each get to have a few minutes off the floor, eat something, go to the bathroom, and maybe take five minutes of fresh air outside.

Admission from the Emergency Room to the Floor

In the hospital, new admissions come to the floor from the emergency room, operating room, special procedure units, or any of the several ICUs. The nurse on the unit from which they are coming usually calls the floor nurse and gives report. The patients who come to the floors from the ER can be from home, transferred from another hospital, from a doctor's office, or from a nursing home. The reporting nurse discusses everything about the patient's medical history, the present diagnosis, current treatments and medications, and the last time the patient was medicated for pain. When the patient arrives on the floor, the nurses make the patient comfortable in bed. If patients are alert and oriented, and it's a two- bed room, the nurses introduce the patient to her/his roommate if there is one. Then they do their physical assessment. This is a head-to-toe assessment covering the patient's cognitive status, vital signs, heart, lungs, abdomen, perineal area, skin, decubiti, lower extremities, and feet. If the patient has dressings, they have to be removed, assessed, and re-dressed. They assess the size of the incisions, staples, or sutures. If there is a decubitus ulcer, the length, width, and depth have to be measured. The decubitus ulcer has to be staged 1, 2, 3, or 4. Knowing the stage of a decubitus ulcer is important in how it is treated. Now they have wound care doctors and nurses who focus only on the decubiti and healing the skin breakdown. Once each week in many nursing homes, the nurses make rounds with a physician from a hospital, who makes recommendations regarding infection control and orders the appropriate medications and dressings for each ulcer that he sees. The recommendations are followed, and in a week, the doctor looks for improvement. Sometimes there is improvement, and other times there is none. The doctor assesses the patient and her/ his nutritional status and sometimes discontinues that treatment and starts something new. This pattern continues until the wound is healed. There are times, however, that the wound does not heal, and the patient has to be admitted to the hospital from the nursing facility for an amputation; or sometimes the patient becomes septic and dies from the complications of the decubitus ulcer. Nurses have to teach the CNAs and PCAs the importance of good skin care, small breaks in the skin, washing, drying, applying lotion, and repositioning the patient. Most patients who have decubitus ulcers are unable to turn themselves, and the entire burden is on you, the caregiver. One cannot overemphasize the importance of nursing care to the debilitated patient, and the importance of the CNAs and PCAs, who most times give showers, baths, and skin care, and turn and reposition the patients in bed.

Documentation of Emergency

Documentation of emergency code situations is extremely important. The time the code was called, the CPR and shock therapy with voltage used, the time 911 came and took over, the drugs used and the time they were administered, the time the doctor was notified, the name of the family member(s) notified, and all other vital information must be recorded. If life support measures were unsuccessful and the patient dies, the time of death will be determined by the 911 doctor who gives the paramedic orders during the code. In some cases during the night if an emergency occurs in a long-term rehab hospital, it is the administrative nursing supervisor who pronounces the patient deceased, after there is no sign of life as per the protocol of the institution. There is no blood pressure, no pulse, and no respiration, and pupils are fixed and dilated. The doctor comes in later and writes the death certificate. This process is allowed only in some states.

However, in the acute care hospital, this is not the case. A doctor is always present. At every code, there is at least one doctor, and during the day, an anesthesiologist is available to intubate the patient. Things are coordinated in the hospital in such a way that the code team is ready to handle any emergency situation. On each shift, nurses are assigned to disaster calls and emergency calls such as codes. If a disaster or emergency is called, that nurse responds to the call. When the code team arrives, the nurse who has been caring for the patient will give the details to the medical team as to whether it was a witnessed arrest or not. The time of the arrest is very important to document, along with the times that various medications were given. It also is important to note the number of times the patient had shock therapy and the various rhythms that were exhibited on the cardiac monitor.

The admission process cannot be overemphasized. Occasionally patients are admitted from home to the nursing home for long-term care, usually when the family can no longer care for them because of the complexity of their medical needs. A decision is made to have them reside in a nursing home. Such a patient, a family member, or the caregiver usually can give you a history of what has been happening to the patient. Many times they forget to take their medications, and when they are admitted, their blood pressure is very high as a result of their noncompliance. Some patients come from home with diabetic ulcers of the feet and blood glucose levels over 300 ml/dl. When the family is told about their blood glucose, they may say that they were unaware that the patient was a diabetic. Many of these new admissions, if they have some type of dementia, as soon as the sun goes down, they become restless and more confused (sundowning syndrome).

Some patients are under the impression that they have to go home to cook, while others may feel they have to lock up the house in preparation for bed. Others will walk off the unit if you are not careful. Some family members fail to mention that their relatives have a history of elopement, which is an important detail to know at the time of admission. If a patient elopes from your institution, the state has to be notified in keeping with guidelines and regulations. These patients are given ankle bracelets to wear that set off an alarm when the patient crosses a door that exits the building. Many skilled care facilities and assisted living facilities now have combination locks for the elevators and doors to prevent patients from getting off the floor.

Census

When the nurse starts her/his tour of duty, it is important to make sure that the census is correct. An incorrect census can cause problems in the billing department, whether it is a Medicaid or a Medicare patient. The patient cannot be in the hospital and in the nursing home at the same time. The census also is important in terms of staffing because units are usually staffed based on the census and the level of care the patients require.

Staffing works well when everyone shows up for work. However, when there are two or three sick calls and you are told by administration not to give overtime because of budgetary constraints, it becomes a big problem. Even if overtime is not an issue, finding staff to replace call-offs can be challenging, to say the least. In order to get someone to work, the supervisor may have to adjust the nursing schedule to meet the nurse's future needs. This happens all the time; however, we have to keep in mind that the patients and their needs come first. Once the units are staffed appropriately, the supervisor can breathe more easily and go about making her/his rounds. S/he can follow up on issues from the last tour and attend to the issues that arise throughout the shift, including changing the schedule of the nurses who came in to help to cover the units.

It can be very challenging for the night nurse if when s/he comes on duty, there is an admission to complete, then s/he has a death, and s/he has a patient that needs to be transferred to the hospital all in the same night. You have to prioritize in terms of what has to be done and in what order. The doctor and next of kin have to be notified when a patient expires, and the time and date have to be accurate. Concise documentation is imperative. It is best for nurses to document things on their working sheet as they go along rather than wait until everything is over to try to remember what happened. This is especially true with cardiac and respiratory arrests. The times are very important.

There are times when you forget to document events; this has happened to all nurses at some time or another in their career.

However, the nurse must call her/his supervisor and inform her/ him of what s/he forgot to document, what drug was given or not given, so that the problem can be addressed immediately. Medications are very important. The following are some important medications: insulins; cardiac drugs such as digoxin; anti- arrhythmic drugs; anticoagulants (Coumadin, heparin); drugs used in the ICU to titrate blood pressure; and those used for blood clots, such as heparin drips. These are just a few examples of medications that can involve serious medical problems if the patient receives a wrong dose or a double dose, or did not receive the medication at all.

Medication Errors

Nurses need to have high moral standards and be of good character because, throughout their careers, they will face many challenges in which honesty and integrity is the best policy. All floor nurses are responsible for administering medications to patients. If you work in specialized areas such as ICUs, the patient-to-nurse ratio is less than that on the floors. On telemetry units, the ratio is more than it is in the ICU, where the nurse-to-patient ratio is usually one nurse to two patients, or sometimes one to three. Nurses who work in an acute care setting on a regular medical, surgical, pediatrics, ob/gyn, or newborn nursery floors have several patients that they have to administer medications to. The nursing home, as opposed to the hospital, sometimes has twenty-five to thirty patients per nurse. Some patients in hospitals and nursing homes get several medications daily. In administering medications, the nurse has to know the brand and generic name of the medication, the correct or usual dosage, how the medications are administered, and possible side effects. On the medication cart, s/he should have a small *Physician's Desk Reference* (PDR) and the current doctor's orders to check before administration of all medications. The patient's medication chart should have the correct name and spelling, allergies, diagnosis, room number, and scheduled times that the medication should be administered. Some hospitals now have an electronic device that scans the patient's wristband for each of the medications administered. This method is effective in that it helps to decrease medication errors. If a medication is missing, the nurse should call the pharmacy and inform them of the missing medication. The pharmacy usually sends it to the floor in a timely manner.

Charting or scanning the patient's wristband without administering the medication is considered a medication error. Some nursing homes use a computerized system but do not have the scanner. Nurses administer the drugs to the patients after checking the 5 R's,(right patient, right medication, right dosage, right route, and right time) and then they chart the medication. Other nursing homes that do not have a computerized system use a medication book. Each patient has a list of medications with the various times that the medications are to be administered. Those patients who are diabetics have to have their glucose testing done three to four times daily, and then they have to be covered with insulin according to the insulin scale as prescribed by the physician, and according to their glucose levels. If a nurse goes off duty and did not chart that insulin was given, the nurse coming on cannot give that insulin. S/he has to call the nurse who went off duty to find out if that medication was given. The supervisor has to be notified. If the nurse forgot to give the medication, it is a medication error. If s/he gave the medication and did not chart it, the supervisor has to be notified, and based on the patient's blood sugar, the doctor also should be notified.

There have been instances when a patient was on several medications, and the nurse charted for the whole week that the medication had been given, but that particular medication was not administered. The drug was not even on the cart, and the pharmacy said that they had not dispensed that particular medication in over a week. Such an instance is a medication error that could lead to disciplinary actions and in some cases, termination of the nurse. Regardless of the circumstances, nurses must be honest and report immediately to the supervisor and doctor if they make a medication error. Ultimately, the patient's life depends on truthful reporting. The nurse must state what was or was not given.

Medical Errors/Adverse Events

According to the Florida Health Care Association in their 2003, revised 2009, literature *Medical Errors: Prevention and Analysis,* medical errors are not the same as medication errors. The Institute of Medicine states the following:

> That medical errors are a failure of a planned action to be completed as intended; or the use of wrong plan to achieve an aim. According to the Agency for Healthcare Research & Policy, medical errors happen when something that was planned as a part of medical care doesn't work out, or when the wrong plan was used in the first place. The Institute of Medicine also says that an "Adverse Event" is an injury resulting from a medical intervention and is not due to the patient's underlying condition. Not all adverse events are attributable to errors.

Some types of medical errors are error or delay in diagnosis; error in the performance of an operation or procedure; error in administering a treatment; failure in communication; equipment failure; and error in dose or method of using a drug, to name a few.

Reporting Requirements in Florida

Skilled care facilities and assisted living facilities are required to report certain incidents. Florida's Risk Management and Quality Assurance Program Reporting System states that there are three categories of reportable events for nursing homes in Florida:

I. Abuse, neglect, and exploitation

II. Avoidable events w/certain outcomes

III. Resident elopement w/certain conditions

Just as nursing homes have regulatory reporting of adverse incidents to the state, the same applies to acute care hospitals. An example of an adverse incident is the death of a patient who was not expected to die. A patient came from a psychiatric institute to the hospital and, at the time of report, was admitted to the floor without a one-to-one caregiver. The patient was admitted for surgery the next day because he swallowed a spoon. Later he was taken to the bathroom by the CNA assigned to him, and as she waited for him right outside the door—which was partially opened—he opened the fourth-floor bathroom window and climbed through, falling to his death. Today, hospital windows are made very secure; some of them cannot be opened, and those that can be opened, can be opened only a few inches.

Another incident that had to be reported to the state involved a patient who walked off the unit and went up the stairs with his

IV and pole, pulled out his IV, and left a trail of blood leading up to the eighth floor. On the eighth floor, he climbed through a window and fell to the ground. He was pronounced dead on the scene. This patient had no psychiatric history documented in his chart, and later the family denied having known of any mental problems.

Another reportable incident involved a patient who fell out of bed while the nurse was caring for him and sustained massive head injury with a lot of bleeding. He later coded and died.

Medical Record Number

All patients are assigned a medical record number once they are admitted to a hospital or nursing facility. That number never changes. It will be the same number used for future admissions, and it is an accurate form of identification within the system. You can have more than one patient with the same name, and occasionally the same date of birth, but never with the same medical record number. At the end of the patient's stay—whether s/he is discharged home, transferred to another facility, or expires—the chart is sent to the medical records department after the whole chart has been audited to make sure that all nurses' notes are signed, all doctors' orders are signed, and the entire chart is complete. These files are usually kept for about seven years in medical records and later are archived. Whenever there is a lawsuit, the administrator of the organization receives a request for medical records or a subpoena to submit the charts. This is why it is so important for all disciplines to complete their notes before the chart is sent to medical records.

Surveys of Hospitals and Nursing Homes

Nurses have to be aware that patients receive funding from Medicare and/or Medicaid to pay some or all of their hospital bills, except for a few patients with private insurance. Medicare and Medicaid have federal and state requirements and standards that have to be met to receive payments and prevent substandard care. The survey process from the state has guidelines, rules, and regulations to ensure that high standards of nursing care are maintained and that policies and procedures are in place to ensure high-quality care. According to *The Long-Term Care State Operations Manual of 2007,*

> Skilled nursing facilities and nursing facilities must be in compliance with the requirements in <u>42 CFR Part 483, Subpart B</u> to receive payment under Medicare or Medicaid. To certify a skilled nursing facility or nursing facility, complete at least:
>
> •A life safety code survey; and,
>
> •A standard survey (<u>Form CMS-670, 671, 672, 677, 801 through 807</u>, and <u>Exhibits 85, 86, 88 to 95</u>).
>
> Following the procedures in Appendix P for conducting all surveys of skilled nursing facilities and nursing facilities, whether freestanding, distinct parts, or dually participating.

Everyone, including the nursing staff, is usually apprehensive during a state survey because the surveyors review all aspects of nursing care, the physical environment, and any issues that the patients may report when they are making rounds or when they sit down to speak with the residents. The surveyors speak to patients, their families if they are visiting, the nurses, the CNAs, the housekeepers, the maintenance crew, the kitchen staff, the administrator, and the director of nursing, and most of all, they read and concentrate on the documentation in the patients' charts. They look at the cleanliness of the institution and the infection control measures, and they focus on the quality and safety of the facility. They review policies and procedures, and then they observe whether those policies and procedures are being carried out. The surveyors observe things such as patients on isolation; infection control procedures; dressing changes; administration of medications; and patients receiving physical therapy, occupational therapy, and recreational therapy. They also observe mealtimes and check whether the meal arrives on time and the temperature of the food at the time of serving. They ask personnel questions. They observe the staff as they feed residents who are unable to feed themselves. The nurses are encouraged to always be professional and welcoming. They should only answer questions asked by the surveyor. If the surveyor asks a question and the staff member does not know the answer, s/he should be confident to tell the surveyor that s/he will get back to her/him with the answer. If the surveyors require copies of any documents, the documents should be given to them and the nursing director should be informed. The survey process usually takes about three to four days, and then there is an exit interview. The team of surveyors, one of which is a registered professional nurse, will then sit in conference with the administrator, the director of nursing, and directors and managers of different services to explain their findings. Based on these findings, the nursing facility will or will not pass the survey. The surveyors have the ability to prevent the hospital or nursing home from receiving new admissions to the facility. If they find that patients are in immediate danger, they can close the facility until such violations are corrected and the facility is in compliance with the regulations of the state.

Pitfalls of Nursing

Nurses work hard. They are conscientious and give continuously of themselves. However, they do not always document what they do for the patients. For all intents and purposes, if an action is not documented in the medical records, it was not done. All nurses' notes must have the date and the time of what was done, instructions given to the patient, the doctor that was notified, and the outcome. One of the major problems with nurses is that they forget to document. This lack of communication causes problems for everyone. In the end, it is the supervisor that the director of nursing will hold responsible, and the state will hold the director of nursing and the administrator responsible.

Another pitfall to avoid is arguing with the doctors in front of other health care members or within earshot of the patients. Discussing your personal life with others at work is not professional. Most people at work are not your friends but your colleagues, and unfortunately, people like to talk. They don't always mean to cause harm, but gossiping about your colleague is not professional. If you have nothing good or uplifting to say about someone, say nothing. Borrowing money from coworkers is unacceptable. Many people like to borrow and not repay, and in some cases, the parties involved end up becoming enemies and stop speaking to each other.

When there is a dispute on the floor, call the supervisor. Inappropriate behavior is unacceptable and is cause for dismissal, especially if it takes place within earshot of the patient. If the supervisor has not yet arrived, do not try to intervene by touching anyone, even in a gentle, nonthreatening manner. This behavior also is unacceptable in the workplace. Touching another person when there is a dispute or argument can be misunderstood. Never get into an argument with a family member. The family can file a complaint against the institution, and they can call the state. The state will come in, and a thorough investigation will be done. It could cost you your job. If you cannot be professional, call the supervisor and tell the family member that you will continue the conversation with your supervisor present. You must always strive to maintain high standards of professionalism.

If a patient falls while care is being administered, it must be reported to the supervisor/manager, doctor, and family, even if the patient does not appear injured in any way. The event must be documented, including an incident report; doctor's order; treatment if any; and the place, date, and time that the incident occurred. This patient should be kept on the report for at least twenty-four hours of continuous monitoring and observation. There have been times when all these things were not done and problems later developed; families get involved and the next thing you know, you have a lawsuit on your hands.

If an incident takes place and you are called to the director's office or the human resources department as part of the investigation, it is best to tell the truth of the entire event as witnessed by you. Do not distort events because the person(s) involved is someone with whom you may have had problems in the past.

If a medication is missing from your cart, do not chart that the medication was given; call the pharmacy, and order the medication. If it is not available, inform the doctor and obtain orders on how to proceed.

Do not leave early and ask a coworker to clock out for you. These are grounds for dismissal. Today, however, a different system is in place. Some institutions require you to check in and out using biometrics— you insert your finger or hand into a machine along with your identification number to clock in and out of work. This has proved to be an effective method of accurately documenting hours worked. If the supervisor calls you in to work at the beginning of a tour and promises you will be paid for the full shift, you still must clock in. A note will be sent to the payroll department asking them to pay you for the entire tour of duty.

When state surveyors are in the building, answer questions to the best of your knowledge. Do not volunteer information. If they ask a question and you do not know the answer, tell them that you will get back to them shortly. Go to your supervisor, get the answer, and get back to them. If they ask you to copy a document, copy the document and give it to them; then inform your supervisor. The state and the Joint Commission of Hospital Accreditation mandate and regulate the standards of care that patients should receive.

Family Complaints

Family complaints happen on a daily basis in all institutions. The complaints are usually wide-ranging, but they are geared toward the nursing care or lack of nursing care that the family perceives their loved one is getting. Once a patient is admitted to the hospital or nursing home, sometimes you can tell immediately that the family will be a challenge, especially for the nursing department. It is best to get to know these families and develop a rapport with them. Offer hospital residents your services, expertise, and teaching to help them throughout their stay in the hospital.

When a family member complains regarding specific aspects of a patient's condition, the complaint has to be addressed immediately. The director of nursing, nurse managers, supervisors, and the doctor should be apprised of the complaint, and steps should be taken to address each issue the family has noted. I have seen families complain about medication that a patient is on, saying that they think that the medication is making their family member worse. Or they complain about certain treatments that the doctor ordered, which, in their opinion, have not helped the family member. In such cases, the doctor has to be informed, and he has to address each issue individually. Sometimes they will discontinue medications or treatments as requested by the family. When this happens, the nursing department must make the changes immediately after consulting with the family and the doctor. The nursing staff must thoroughly document the interventions taken to resolve issues. The family should be kept updated about what the doctors and nurses are doing for their family, and everything should be discussed until the families are satisfied and issues are resolved.

When complaints such as these arise, the director of nursing and the entire health-care team should look at the patient's diagnosis and all the doctor's orders to make sure that everything is appropriate for the patient. For example, if the patient is debilitated and malnourished, he may need to have total parenteral nutrition (TPN). If he has a decubitus ulcer, he will need an air mattress, and care will be provided by the wound care doctor. If the patient's extremities are showing atrophy, we have to make sure that the patient is getting the appropriate occupational and physical therapy to restore the patient to optimum health. The dietician should be involved to monitor weight gain or loss. The nurses should report all changes, even the subtle ones, to the doctor in order to improve the patient's condition. Social service should be involved. Involvement of the entire team usually has positive outcomes.

In many cases, once a rapport is developed with the family and they see that the entire staff is doing the best that they can, they become less apprehensive. Some families, however, will go to the extreme and notify the state and complain that the hospital or the nursing home has not addressed their complaints or has done nothing about them. Many times, the state will visit the institution to investigate the allegations.

A sentinel event is an unexpected occurrence that can involve death or serious physical or psychological injury. All of these injuries must be reported to the state by the risk manager, the director of nursing, or the administrator. An example of this could be a patient falling off a bed and sustaining massive head injuries while the bed was in a high position. Another example could be a patient who dies, becomes paralyzed, or goes into a coma due to a medication error. Another example could be the suicide of a patient who comes from a psychiatric institute into an acute care hospital, is assigned a one-to-one caregiver, and still climbs through a window to his death. Another example might be the elopement of a patient who crosses a busy interstate highway, is seriously injured, and is placed on life support. A surgical procedure could be done on the wrong patient, or the wrong organ or limb might be removed; or a death could result from an infection acquired in the hospital. These are just some examples of sentinel events.

In a small rehab hospital, one of the responsibilities of the director of nursing is to sit with the pharmacist in a closed area and destroy unused narcotics and controlled drugs. These drugs are then safely disposed of using protocol as per the policy of the institution. The director of nursing also is involved in customer satisfaction surveys, performance improvement, and employee retention. Most of all, the director of nursing should be professional, warm, and compassionate toward the patients. S/he is their advocate, and s/he keeps her/his patients safe at all costs; s/he keeps the staff educated with current knowledge of their professional responsibilities to care for the patients.

Intimate Knowledge
Gained as a Nurse

ICU Staff Nurse—St. Mary's Hospital

My first week in the surgical ICU was very devastating for me. To begin with, quite a few of my classmates wanted to work in the ICU, but only a few of us got the opportunity. I did very well with my clinical evaluation in medical/surgical units. I was one of three in my class that made the dean's list in my second year in nursing school after I completed my required courses at Monroe Community College. St. Mary's Hospital was affiliated with the college at that time. On one particular day in the unit, I made rounds with the attending physician for my patient. At the bedside, he discussed changing the dose of a medication she was already taking. He gave me a verbal order, and I wrote it on my work sheet, went to the medication room to retrieve the medication, and administered the medication to the patient. Before he left the unit, I went to look at the chart to pick up the order. The doctor had written a different dosage. I felt scared, but

I spoke to him and told him that he had made a mistake because that was not the dosage he had ordered at the patient's bedside. My supervisor was right there with me. I was truly terrified. All I could think was that I was going to be fired. Eventually, the doctor admitted that he had given me that order but had changed his mind after looking over the chart. He then wrote a one-time order for the dose I had given, but the supervisor still disciplined me by writing me up. I could have gotten into so much trouble had I not looked at the orders before the doctor left the unit. I thank God for saving me and thank him that the doctor did admit to telling me to give that dosage. However, that was a lesson I have never forgotten since 1971. Since then, I have refused to take verbal orders while the doctor was present on the floor, except in a code situation. I always say to the doctors that I'll be happy to give the mediations as soon as they write it.

New graduates on orientation especially should abide by this rule. If the doctor is on the floor and it is not a code situation, do not take verbal orders. Wait until the order is written! Since that day, I have been extremely careful with doctor's orders and medications. Over the years, I have educated nurses in that regard. Doctors can change their minds between the time they leave the bedside and the time they walk to the nursing station. I was lucky I had a doctor who was professional and honest.

The ICU has very sick patients. We had some on ventilators about whom I felt uncertain, even though I knew the principles of what the ventilator did for the patients, and what the various settings meant. But being a new nurse, I had my fears. Eventually, after a few months I began to get comfortable and could even be left alone for a few minutes in the unit. Gaining confidence in my work was very important for me, and early on it was clear that I could take charge and make the correct decisions for my patients. I had my finger on the pulse in terms of what was going on with them. I must tell you, it was an exhilarating feeling—far, far from my first week in the ICU.

Staff Nurse/Floor—The New York Hospital Medical Center of Queens (formally Booth Memorial)

In 1972, I moved from Rochester, New York, to Queens to be near my family. I had just had one baby and had found out I was expecting my second. I worked on a very busy forty-five-bed acute care orthopedic unit in the hospital on the 3 to 11 tour. I loved nursing. Caring for my patients was everything to me. I looked forward to going to work. By now, I was a mentor to many nurses who would come and ask me to show them various nursing procedures. It was wonderful! I worked hard. Many days there were no breaks or lunchtime, but I loved my job. Patients were mostly postoperative from the day tour or a few days before. There were many pre-op patients who had to have surgery the next day. The doctors wanted patients up and out of bed the day after surgery, so there was a lot of physical work to get patients into and out of bed. One of the things that I learned was that you must have help to get your patients into and out of bed. Sometimes patients faint while you are getting them from the bed to a chair or vice versa. Even though you use good body mechanics, one person is not enough to help postop patient in transferring Always have enough help available to avoid accidents and incidents. Patient safety is paramount, especially in the hospital or nursing home. Teach patients how to get up and pivot to get from the bed to the chair, using the techniques taught to them by physical and occupational therapists. On a busy unit such as this, there were very sick patients who were nauseated, sometime vomiting, with IVs and Foley catheters. They all needed close monitoring of vital signs, observation for bleeding from operative sites, and pain medication to keep them comfortable and free of pain.

Nursing Supervisor

Working as an administrative nursing supervisor at a two-hundred-bed nursing facility was my first experience as a supervisor. I started on days, and I had to get used to the environment of the nursing home. There were no doctors walking around and nursing running up and down the halls. It was an elderly population, and nursing assistants (formerly called nurse's aides) were giving nursing care and taking patients to and from therapy. In that capacity I had to do a lot of teaching, especially to the nursing assistants. As I would go from floor to floor and look at the reports and the temperature sheets, I often noticed most of the patients' vital signs were 98.6°F, 72/20. Sometimes I challenged the recordings, and to my dismay the written documentation was not always accurate. As a result, the assistants were taught the correct way to do vital signs, to document, and to observe and report to the charge nurse.

On the day tour, the supervisor covered two units, but on evenings, she covered the entire building. This was very rewarding for me because, at this point in my career, I felt comfortable; I was able to make decisions on my own and function independently. Staffing was a problem for me then because, when nurses would call in sick, I had to spend time trying to get replacements, while also dealing with the various nursing issues that were arising on the floors. As a result, I was always busy. However, patients received excellent nursing care under my leadership, and the nurses and nursing assistants felt very comfortable coming to me for assistance and guidance. I got to know the families and had a good rapport with most of them.

Clinician/Supervisor—Surgical Unit, 1,200-Bed Municipal Hospital

Having had three years' experience as an ICU nurse, an orthopedic nurse on a busy forty-five-bed acute care unit, and a nursing supervisor in a two-hundred-bed nursing home made me confident to apply for a position as clinician nursing supervisor on the surgical service in Queens Hospital Center. Soon after I got this job, my supervisor, the assistant director of nursing, asked me to assist in updating the policy and procedure manual for the surgical service. She was pleased with my performance. Initially, I was both excited and nervous. My main function, however, was to teach the young nurses how to make the transition from orientation to the floor. Many of the nurses were scared, uncertain, and sometimes overwhelmed like I was initially. Their first days and weeks on the unit were a struggle. Many said they had no idea nursing was so intense and in-depth. We would have conferences on a daily basis after their assignments and after certain procedures. The nurses were encouraged to make their needs known and to verbalize their fears and concerns. After a few weeks, however, most of them were able to function independently, knowing that they had someone to reach out to for information and assistance as needed. Nurses were taught on the surgical service that no question was ever stupid. The rule was if they were not sure, they must ask because of their responsibility for human lives. Nurses were encouraged to share information and to help each other. We provided a buddy system for them even after they graduated from their preceptor. They needed to know that they could check with a more-senior nurse if they had any questions about things such as giving regular and long-acting insulin, which insulin could be mixed, and which should be pulled up first. If they were not sure how to give subcutaneous (SC) or intramuscular (IM) injections, they could call on any of the other nurses, who would gladly share their knowledge with them and not look at them in a negative light or criticize them in any way. In calculation of medication dosages, new orientees felt comfortable asking for help when they were not sure.

The nurse should be able to look and observe subtle changes in her/his patients, monitor them, and inform the physician of their findings. S/he has to know that when s/he calls the doctor, s/he has the latest vital signs and knows exactly what is taking place with her/his patient. S/he has to be able to make split-second decisions at times in order to save the life of a patient. In everything that the nurse does, s/he has to prioritize. What must I do first? Which is more important? Out of all that is happening, which of these things can wait? These are just some of the questions that you process while working with your patient. Comforting the patient is paramount. Educating the patients about their illnesses is very important, and helping them do as much as they can for themselves is great therapy for recovery. Giving them hope is what nurses do for all their patients.

On rounds with the physician in the mornings, encourage the patients to ask the doctors questions that they have verbalized to you earlier. Patients have a tendency to smile with the physician when he comes in, and to say things that are not truly relevant to what is happening or to what they should be asking. Encourage patients to ask physicians to change pain medications that are ineffective, and to ask them to give them the correct dosage to control their pain. Encourage them to ask important questions that they have about their condition. Patients from some cultures do not want to ask the doctor questions directly; they prefer to go through the nurse. Somehow, they feel it would question the doctor's authority. There should be no need to call the physician right after he has seen a patient.

Coughing, deep breathing, moving in bed, and getting up and out of bed are extremely important to prevent post-op complications such as pneumonia and embolism (blood clot). In my work as a clinician, policy and procedure manuals were reviewed almost daily to get the new nurses to start out with good nursing practices that would stay with them throughout their careers. Encourage them to use these manuals often and to give nursing care based on the nursing standards of the policies and procedures for the institution where they work, always striving for excellence. When policies are updated or changed, meetings are held to inform the nursing staff of any and all procedure changes.

The nurse clinician should get to know her/his staff. S/he should know their weaknesses and areas of expertise. They should be praised and thanked when they do outstanding jobs. If they don't do such an outstanding job, then the clinician should review with them what they need to do to become competent in the particular area that needs improvement.

Nurses have to be educators. The nurse needs to be confident. When talking with her/his patient, s/he should have full knowledge of all the drugs s/he administers to them so s/he can teach them when the medications should be taken. Some medications should be taken on an empty stomach, some before meals, and some after meals. Some specifically should be taken with food in order to get the optimum results from the drug. S/he has to be aware of drug interactions and reactions, and s/he must know all medications that the patient is allergic to. If the patient is alert and oriented, the patient should be asked if s/he has allergies. If the patient is confused, you must check the chart. Nurses must constantly teach their patients.

At the time of the evaluation period, the nurse clinician should have a good knowledge of the kind of nurse that the orientee is and will become. Evaluations have to be open, candid, and honest. In ensuring this, the nurse will become better in her/his nursing practice. The nurse has to be able to communicate clearly with the doctors and her/his peers. S/he has to articulate to the physician exactly and as accurately as possible what is happening to the patient. As was stated before, the nurse should have current vital signs and the exact reason for calling the physician, along with the latest blood glucose level if the patient is diabetic. S/he should have recent lab results for that day and knowledge of the lab results for the day before. If the patient is on a cardiac monitor, the nurse must be able to read the rhythm the patient is in, and know the medication that is being taken, and the time and dose the medication was last administered. S/he also should be able to convey to the doctor the requests of the patient and/or the patient's next of kin.

Patients' families can play an important role in their recovery and outcome. It's important at the beginning of the tour for the nurse to know the names and primary diagnosis of all her/his patients. S/he should have a list of her/his diabetic patients, and those who are DNR and do not intubate (DNI) . S/he should have a list of her/his pre- and post-op patients, those with epilepsy, those that are confused, those that climb out of bed, and those that tend to wander. The nurse should check if the patients are wearing their wander guards and if the guards are in working condition. Safety is the number one priority for all patients. Those patients on fall precautions, those with decubitus ulcers, those who are incontinent, and those who require turning and repositioning every two hours should be monitored carefully. S/he should make sure that all her/ his patients are wearing their identification wristband, and the spelling of the name must be correct. When a patient is transferred to a hospital or other facility, the correct wristband can determine how quickly that patient is treated in the ER. A confused patient from a nursing home with no wristband cannot be treated until her/his identity is established by a nurse from the institution from which they are being transferred. Many times, nurses have to take a taxi from the nursing home to the hospital, to bring the patient's identification and allergy bands to the hospital before the doctors will treat the patient. Of course, in an emergency such as a cardiac or respiratory arrest, this would not be the case.

Nurses have to be aware and exercise the HIPAA law when giving information to family members on the telephone. Many hospitals have developed systems to let hospital personnel know whom they are speaking to through the use of a code that is given to the next of kin and those to whom the patient wants information given. Some family members try to argue with the nurse, telling her/him that they are close family who have a right to know. Again, the nurse has to explain the HIPAA law to the family member and tell her/him that the next of kin has all the needed information. You also can refer the family member to the physician for further information.

All families should be treated with respect, empathy, and dignity. You have to step out of your nursing hat and put yourself in their place and try to understand if you had a loved one in the hospital, how you would feel. In most cases, these families are not nurses or doctors. Everything is not always easy for them to understand. Sometimes families come across angry and anxious, and many times, that's just how they feel. They tend to vent their feelings on the nurse. Nurses have to understand this and know not to take it personally. Try to help the family cope as best as possible. Take a minute and let them talk. LISTEN. Offer them coffee, tea or juice, sit with them in a private lounge area. Try to develop a rapport with them. Always maintain high ethical standards with the patients and their families regardless of how they behave. Remember, they are anxious and frightened of the outcome of their loved ones.

Private Duty Nurse

Private duty nursing can be defined as one nurse taking care of one patient in a hospital, nursing home, assisted living facility, or home. In 1980, working as a nursing supervisor in a very large hospital, I was introduced to private duty nursing after speaking with one of the floor nurses. The opportunity seemed lucrative, and that type of one-to-one nursing was not as stressful as managing several acute care units. Most of these patients are wealthy, and unlike the patients on the floor, they expect a lot more from you. In terms of nursing care, when you come on duty, you receive report from the nurse going off duty. These patients are not in ICU or special care units. They usually are in a private or semiprivate room on the floors. The patients can range from being very sick, on the ventilator, or they can be postoperative patients or patients ambulating in the halls who need minimal assistance.

Personality is vitally important in doing private duty nursing. You can be fired by the patient because s/he doesn't like you for whatever reason. Some feel that you are not qualified, because you did not use the same technique during a nursing procedure that the nurse before you used, even though neither nurse was wrong. Some patients do not like it when you wear perfume. Some patients don't want to see you sit down. They may want you to be busy all the time. Some patients get annoyed because you spend a bit of time out of the room, even when you explain to them that you have to check the doctor's orders and that there are many things that you have to do at the nursing station. Such things may include picking up doctor's orders, writing nursing notes, and preparing medications. Many patients like to have a private duty nurse because of the company, and they feel more secure and safe. Overall, many of these patients just want to know that they have a nurse that they can call on and that their needs can be taken care of immediately. A good example of this would be that they don't have to wait for their pain medication or for a bath. They can ask for whatever they want, even to take another bath even though they received a bath on the shift before you came on. If they do not want the food that has been sent up for them, the nurse can immediately call down to the kitchen without there being a long waiting period.

Many of these patients have been told that they can call the doctor directly and that s/he will return their call to answer any questions they may have. The doctor, however, usually calls back at the nursing station, where the nurse takes the orders for any changes in nursing care or changes in medication. Private duty nurses are under the direct supervision of another registered professional nurse who is on staff at the hospital. Ultimately, the hospital nurse is directly in charge of the private duty nurse. The hospital nurse will inform the private duty nurse immediately of any emergencies or any changes that the doctor makes. Some hospitals do not allow the private duty nurses to pick up orders. That is, the doctor has to speak to the nurse covering the floors to give her/him the order. In some institutions, the doctor writes the order in the computer, the floor nurse transcribes the order, and the private duty nurse carries out the order.

There are times when the doctor comes in to examine the patient, and the patient asks you to step outside. After the doctor leaves, whether or not you are told anything, the private duty nurse must always check the chart to see if the doctor changed any medications or ordered something new.

Some of these patients are on isolation, and the patient has to be treated by using the protocols of the institution. Infection control is extremely important. Proper hand washing is the most effective method to prevent the spread of disease. This cannot be overemphasized. The patient's safety is very important. A confused patient who is likely to climb out of bed or pull out tubing cannot be left alone. The private duty nurse must speak with the staff nurse who is covering her/him if s/he needs to leave the room. In some cases, the staff nurse has to bring in the medication and administer it to the patient.

One evening on the 4-to-12 shift, I was walking down the halls and in an open private room I saw a patient in a recliner with blood gushing out onto the floor. I yelled for help, pulled the sheet off the bed, and helped to stop the bleeding. He was coded and then taken to the OR. I later learned that he was a second-day post-op patient. The patient could have been on isolation. I did not stop to think. I just reacted to save the patient, who survived.

Private duty nursing at Mount Sinai was an exciting time for me. It was my part-time job, which helped me a great deal financially. Most of my experiences were positive ones, and I have made lasting friendships with some of my patients. It was because of private duty nursing that I had the distinct privilege and honor to meet two presidents of the United States, who are still living today. The first happened when I was assigned to care for Mr. Lionel Hampton. He was a world-renowned jazz musician, and I was his nurse at Mount Sinai. He was featured in the *New York Post* newspaper as I accompanied him home from the hospital along with a friend from the governor's office.

One day at home, a call came in for Mr. Hampton. I answered the phone and asked who was calling, and the caller said, "George Bush."

I said, "George Bush! President Bush?"

He said, "Yes." We spoke for a few seconds before Mr. Hampton came to the phone. I later learned that they were good friends and that Mr. Hampton was a true Republican, always attending important events held by the party. Mr. Hampton met my husband and children, and we became like family to him over the years. He spent many Thanksgiving holidays at our home in Queens. He was godfather to my daughter's first child, and we visited each other's homes. He would call me at home late sometimes if he had any medical concerns, just to hear my opinion. He told me that he valued my opinion very much.

When Mr. Hampton died, President Bush and my family were in the same room at the same time because both of our limousines arrived at the door of the church at the same time. The president was in front. We were led into the same room; however, about ten minutes later, the Secret Service asked us if we were with the president's entourage. I said no. I did not get to speak with President Bush then because he was speaking to the governor and other officials. We were led into the church before the president. The service was joyful. It was a celebration of his life, and we as a family missed him along with people around the world.

On another occasion, a friend and colleague from Mount Sinai private duty staff invited me to a luncheon for business executives on Long Island. The guest speaker was President Bill Clinton. After the luncheon ended, the president left the stage.

I told my friend and those sitting at our table that I wanted to meet the president. They laughed and said he had already left. I was determined to speak with him, so I walked all the way across the auditorium and came up on a crowd. I made my way to the middle of the gathering. There I saw President Clinton engaged in a conversation with a reporter. He was trying desperately to get away. As I moved closer to him, I heard him tell the reporter that he had to go now. As he turned to leave, I pushed forward in the crowd. I was wearing a red dress, so I stood out. In a loud voice I said, "Mr. President," and he looked back as I held out my hand over the crowd. He smiled and shook my hand. Then he was gone. He is a lot better-looking in person than on TV.

Overall, private duty nursing can be very rewarding, as it has been for me. One incident that comes to mind is once when I walked into a patient's room, and he had a tray in front of him. He started eating and began to choke. I was there to help this patient, who had suffered a stroke. He was to be evaluated by the speech pathologist for swallowing reflexes. The tray had been placed on his table, and he started eating. I still had my coat on, had not yet received report from the nurse, and actually saved the patient from choking. Another time, I was taking care of a patient who had just been transferred from the ICU after cardiac bypass surgery. The patient was still unstable. It gave me great joy to nurse that patient back to the point where he could eventually ambulate in the halls. To see such a patient go home brings such joy and satisfaction to my soul. I enjoyed working as a private duty nurse because I learned so much from my patients; I also had the opportunity to teach them many things, such as good hand-washing practice, taking medications as prescribed, following up with doctor's visits, and eating healthfully. I talked to them about their diagnosis and how to stay healthy. Over the years, I have taken care of hundreds of patients, and I could tell you many stories. Thank God, most of them are positive.

Surgical Admission Planner

When I worked as a surgical admission planner, we were always on the telephone with the doctors or nurses from the doctors' offices scheduling surgeries. They would tell you the date they wanted, and we would then let them know about the availability of the date and time. In scheduling surgeries, the nurse has to consider how long repairing a simple, uncomplicated hernia would take as opposed to performing open-heart surgery, and the number of bypass grafts that would be involved. The time needed for the surgeon to complete each case is an important consideration in order to schedule each patient. We scheduled all types of operations, except for neurosurgeries. Preventing overbooking was important in case something went wrong and the surgeon needed more time. All patients going for surgery were always kept NPO as of midnight prior to the surgery. When there was a delay, these patients could become a problem, especially if they were diabetic. Physicians were sometimes too tired, or they could become ill during a surgery, and the next case had to be canceled.

Home-Care Coordinator

In my role as nursing coordinator in a large home-care agency affiliated with the same twelve-hundred-bed hospital, we had what we called intake coordinators and home-care coordinators. I started out as an intake coordinator. I would see the patients prior to discharge and speak with them and their families regarding their concerns about going home. They would have an RN, physical therapist (PT), occupational therapist (OT), and home health aide as ordered by the physician and according to their insurance plan. Then we would arrange for all the medical equipment the patient would need at home, such as a hospital bed, bedside table, commode, walker, cane, and shower chair. These are examples of some of the needs that a patient being discharged from the hospital to home would need. However, we would always have to check with the insurance company to see what they were willing to pay for, and if the family was prepared to pay for the rest. Those patients on Medicaid would be given supplies that Medicaid allowed.

Home-care patients are patients that are discharged from the hospital and are receiving skilled nursing care at home. In home care, each coordinator would have fifty to seventy patients under her/his care. A small percentage would be high-tech patients with intravenous TPN. There also were noncompliant patients who refused to take their medications as ordered or refused to participate in physical or occupational therapy as required to stay in the home-care program. Some patients needed a home visit from the coordinator in charge of their case. They were very happy to see that someone in charge came to see them. Some, even with home visits, were still noncompliant, and we had to inform the doctor, the family, and the insurance carrier and take them off service. We left guidelines for their safety and recovery, and we contacted the next of kin to help them deal with the problems. We left telephone numbers to call the doctor or emergency help before taking them off service. Some of these patients would return to the agency with a different attitude, and the agency, given the circumstances, would take them back on service.

Patients going home on oxygen must be told, along with the family, that no smoking can take place in the house. The patient might need skilled care at home from a registered nurse, physical therapist, and an occupational therapist, depending on the patient's needs and health insurance. All these arrangements are made before the time of discharge. At the time of a patient's discharge, the primary doctor must be notified and given a list of the current medications that the patient is going home with, and the same is faxed to his office. This prevents mistakes if the doctor is not present at the hospital on the day of discharge. Medications are reviewed with the patient if s/he is alert and oriented, and also with the family member the patient is being discharged to. They are given the doctor's telephone number for clarification of questions regarding medications and other questions they might have.

The most important thing at the time of discharge is that the discharge plan is a safe one and that the patient will be able to function at her/his optimum level with the plan in place. Prior to discharge, the patient must be given clear instructions regarding medications and communication with the doctor. The nurse must review the care plan with the patient and the caregiver who will be supervising the patient's care at home. Emergency numbers should be listed, including those for the doctor and the hospital, with the floor number and extension of the nurses' station that the patient is discharged from. Therefore, when patients get home, they can call and speak with the nurse directly if they have a question. Today this is called case management. They discuss with the physician the level of care the patient will need from the hospital. Some patients require long-term rehab hospitalization—usually those patients have multiple systems complications or multiple systems failure, and whose family do not wish to sign a DNR order or put the patient on hospice. In some cases, putting a patient on hospice is hard for the family, such as with a patient who is on dialysis three times per week who has end-stage renal failure. Many of these patients cannot survive more than a week without dialysis, as they would go into uremic coma and die. Nurses have to be understanding and not be judgmental on these cases, because these kinds of decisions are hard to make.

Once the patient goes home, the home-care nurses and therapists make their visits and set up a plan of care with the patient and family. When I was a home-care coordinator with a caseload of over sixty patients years ago, the RNs, physical therapists, and occupational therapists would call in and update the coordinator on the patients' condition. This would include reports such as the patient went to the ER over the weekend with reason stated; the patient was admitted back into the hospital; medications were changed due to a change in condition; the family needs more help in the home; the patient did not keep his doctor's appointment; or the aide told the nurse that the patient had a loaded gun under his pillow. When confronted, the patient might have been uncooperative because the gun was not licensed, and this would have to be reported to the police, and in some cases the state. The home-care coordinator would notify the doctor and the next of kin that services were being terminated because of an unsafe environment. The family would be advised to seek counseling for the patient as needed.

In some cases, the patient refuses to take medications as ordered by the physician. This can create an unsafe environment for the patient and the nurse, especially with psychiatric patients. Their behavior can become very bizarre and dangerous, requiring readmission to the hospital.

Sometimes the coordinator pays the patient a surprise visit to observe the care that the professionals and the home health aide are giving, and to see if the patient is compliant. A visit also gives the coordinator an idea of the relationship the patient has with the home health aide, the nurse, and the therapist. There are times that a patient makes complaints that ordinarily s/he would not make over the telephone. These complaints are investigated, and if they are valid, then appropriate changes are made. In some high-tech cases in which patients are very ill, they do not have a DNR order and can afford nurses. These patients have nurses around the clock that are supplemented by their own insurance or paid for by the family. Some patients are diagnosed with terminal cancer and are malnourished and continue to lose weight. In these cases, the doctor sometimes puts the patient on TPN, which has to be administered by using a central line that has to be assessed and monitored by a registered professional nurse. Patients whose families are involved in their care depend on the nurses to educate them about what to do in their absence. Infection control is emphasized. They are taught good hand-washing technique to use before and after touching the insertion site dressings. Sometimes these patients are diabetic, and for those that that don't have nurses, but have a family member that is a caregiver, the caregiver is educated on how to administer insulin injections subcutaneously. After teaching them, the nurses usually lets the caregiver do a return demonstration with sterile normal saline. The nurses educate the family about the medications, their uses, side effects, adverse reactions to the drugs, and anaphylactic shock, which can occur with various medications. I have seen seizures happen soon after a drug is administered. Families have to be taught what to do, including calling 911 if there is an emergency. The home-care department makes more visits and does random audits to make sure that everyone is in compliance with the policies and procedures of the hospital's home-care agency. State regulations are always adhered to with all patients, especially those who are very sick.

While I was working as a home-care coordinator, a state survey was conducted during August 15–19, 1991, and the state used a number of my patients' charts. In their exit interview, the state inspectors said, "Home Care Coordinator Jean McGrath was identified as one … whose charts reflected the most complete and thorough follow-up of identified problems."

Assistant Director of Nursing— Nursing Home

As an assistant director of nursing in a nursing home, I was involved with staff education and infection control. I also was involved in the day-to-day planning of the nursing department. This included making rounds, dealing with family complaints, dealing with the nurses and nursing assistants, making sure that the patients were receiving the proper nursing care, and making sure that the patients on isolation were in isolation rooms with isolation protocols and that they were receiving the appropriate care. Good hand-washing technique was practiced and emphasized on a daily basis because, as most people know, it is the most effective way to prevent transmission of diseases from one patient to another.

Each day, staffing for that day and the next few days had to be looked at carefully to make sure that the nursing home was staffed sufficiently to provide and maintain the best possible nursing care for each resident. This is based on the census and the acuity of the patients. Staffing the units with qualified nursing professionals is important to meet the nursing needs for the residents' physical and psychological well-being. During the course of the day, staff that called in sick had to be replaced before the change of shift in order to maintain a smooth transition to the next shift. In some states, if staffing goes below a certain ratio, the institution can be fined by the state, and the institution will not be able to take in any new admissions. Again, as was mentioned before, the institution could be put on moratorium.

In this position as assistant director of nursing, I had to approve vacations, requested time off, and requested leaves of absence; assist the committee implementing policies and procedures; sit in on new-hire interviews; and sit in with the director of nursing in meetings regarding patient care, day-to-day operations, and state regulations. I was involved with disciplinary actions and disciplinary hearings, which included dealing with unions. I would be involved with the nurse educator to demonstrate the use of new equipment that the facility would purchase from time to time. I was the person to fill in the director's shoes when she was not present or was unavailable. In that role, I got to know the staff, the patients, and their families on a personal level.

Administrative Supervisor

Working in a twelve-hundred-bed hospital with several acute care units, I was in charge of several units. If I covered the emergency room, that alone was three units: the adult ER, pediatrics ER, and psych ER. Other medical units included pediatric units, ICUs,

OR, recovery, newborn nursery, premature ICU (now called neonatal ICU, NICU), and labor and delivery. Depending on how many supervisors were on duty, we would divide the hospital units among ourselves. However, whoever covered the ER never covered ICU. The division of the units would start from the ICU to the OR.

As a young student nurse, I had the opportunity to observe a few days of surgery in the operating room with different doctors, different surgeries, and the various nurses working with them. This was a long time ago, but I recall the team being very organized. Everyone in the room was sterile. Their hands, gowns, masks, and gloves were sterile. At that time, I remember what they called a "circulating nurse." She made sure that all the instruments the surgeon needed were laid out on a sterile table for him to perform the operation. The anesthesiologist stayed at the head of the patient's table to monitor the intubation tube and vital signs. There was a count of every instrument and every 4x4 dressing used, and at the end of the surgery, the count would be done again before the patient was closed. It was especially important that nothing was left inside the patient that did not belong there. During this time the surgeons portrayed completely different personalities. Some of them were funny, while others were harsh and unprofessional. At times, especially when things were not going well, you had to have thick skin to work in the OR. It was there for the first time that I saw what cancer looked like.

While making rounds as an administrative supervisor covering the emergency room on the 3 to 11 shift along with other units, I witnessed a gunshot wound of a male patient brought in by ambulance. The patient was taken to the OR almost immediately. IV access was gained, and normal saline was hung wide open; bloods were drawn for type and cross match, and then he was transported to the OR. The wound was abdominal. In the OR, the surgeons started to work, and they were able to control the bleeding. I saw the doctors lift and examine the entire intestines, one segment at a time; first one doctor checked, then the next doctor, and then the next. It was shocking for me! I left after about an hour when all the staff was in place and things were a little more settled. I was being paged by other units that needed me. I can't recall the outcome of the surgery, but that was a frightening experience for me—seeing so much blood and hearing everyone shouting orders, and the OR nurses performing at their best, working with the doctors to save the patient's life. These are experiences you never, ever forget! It was shocking for me! I had not seen surgery since I was a student nurse.

These are experiences that you never forget. Just as I never forgot on my way to school, at Mary Mount Manhattan College, to take my final exam in statistics (early 1980s) a passenger went into cardiac arrest on the train. I performed cardiopulmonary resuscitation (CPR) until another person joined in to help. It seemed like 911 rescue took forever! When they came, however, the passenger was still alive. I got to class late and did poorly on my exam, but I passed the course. In spite of it all, I felt good because I had made a difference in helping to save a life.

Emergency surgeries are not planned, but doctors, nurses, OR technicians, and anesthesiologists all have to be ready, on call in the hospital. There is usually a waiting room for the family to wait to hear the outcome of the surgery. The room is usually clean and comfortable, with coffee, tea, and a bathroom. Today, some waiting rooms have a television screen with the patient's name, the doctor's name, the time the surgery started, and the expected time that the patient will be out of surgery.

The anesthesia the patient receives—such as general anesthesia, monitored anesthesia care (MAC), or epidural block—affects how long it will be before the patient becomes fully awake. The surgeon usually comes to the room and speaks with the next of kin, such as the wife, husband, parent, or close relatives. Once the family is told the surgery went well, they are relieved. However, sometimes the news is not what was anticipated. In those instances, the doctor takes the family to a private room, sits with them, and explains what happened. Things don't always turn out well, but God always knows best.

The assistant director of nursing was away on vacation for a month. It was quite an honor that she asked me, a junior supervisor, to cover the hospital in her absence. I acted in the capacity of nurse administrator, covering the entire hospital on the 3-to-11 tour with several other supervisors under my leadership. This was an exciting time for me and my colleagues. We worked very well together, keeping each other informed. When the assistant director of nursing returned, she was pleased with our performance.

Later, at this same institution, I worked only weekends on the day tour with another colleague, each of us covering half of the hospital, from the emergency room to the operating room on the tenth floor. These were all acute care units.

Working in the Bronx in a 240-bed skilled care facility, I worked in the same capacity as an administrative nursing supervisor. At this facility, I was in charge of the entire nursing home on the 3-to- 11 tour. My responsibilities were much different from the same position in the hospital. I had to make sure that the floors were properly staffed. Whenever I arrived on duty, I would take report from the director of nursing and the managers from each floor. I would do the narcotic count for the nursing office, and then I would make rounds on all the floors. I would speak with all the managers if possible to find out if there were pressing issues that had to be dealt with immediately and if follow-ups needed to be done. I would make rounds and see most of the patients. Some of them were not on the floors, because they were still in physical therapy, out on a doctor's appointment, out on pass with family, or out for dialysis. I had to make sure when they came back to the facility, that those patients were assessed for any change in condition by the RN. Most of the admissions came in on the evening tour, and so did the visitors.

Although each floor had two nurses, the census on each floor ranged from thirty to fifty-four patients, so the nurses were extremely busy. It was the responsibility of the supervisor to assess and admit the patients; on admission the supervisor had to speak with the attending physician and review the orders with the doctor. Then the orders were submitted to the pharmacy. The medications would be delivered couple hours after the orders were submitted. For those patients who were on tube feeding, the dietary department was notified, and the tube feeding would be brought up to the floor. If patients needed BIPAP machines before going to the nursing homes, they were usually ordered in the hospital. In regard to making rounds, the nurses were always taught to make sure the narcotic count was correct before taking responsibility for the floor, to take report from the nurse going off duty, and then to give report to the CNAs. The nurses then had to check the emergency cart for oxygen, a functioning suctioning machine, a CPR board, gloves, and emergency medications as per the protocol of the institution. All patients on oxygen were checked to make sure that they were not still receiving oxygen from the small portable oxygen tanks. Nurses were instructed to take patients off the oxygen tanks and to connect the tubing to the oxygen concentrator or the oxygen flowing through the wall. CNAs also were instructed to always check their patients on oxygen to make sure that the nasal cannula and tubing were kept clean and patent (clear and without obstruction). Special care had to be given to those patients receiving oxygen so that their nose did not become crusty and sore.

On a daily basis, safety and pain management were emphasized. For those patients on tube feedings, the CNAs were reminded that the head of the bed had to be kept at least at a forty-five-degree angle to prevent aspiration pneumonia, and when giving care they had to first call the nurse to turn off the tube feeding. Even then, the head of the patient's bed was never to be flat. This was a safety precaution to prevent aspiration of tube feeding. All nursing standards of the institution and the state were adhered to.

Staffing for the oncoming shift had to be checked at the beginning of the tour and throughout the tour of duty. Employees who were absent or called in sick during that shift had to be replaced before the beginning of the next shift. Nurses who had to attend in-service education classes had to arrange with the other nurse on the floor to take over while they attended classes. Continuing mandatory in-service education was always a priority in keeping each nurse current with the standards of nursing care. There were times when state representatives would be in the house. They would arrive starting early in the morning, and sometimes at 6 p.m., they would still be in-house. I was interviewed a few times by representatives from the state regarding different complaints that they came to investigate. It was my responsibility to cooperate with the representatives and work corroboratively with the entire health-care team to improve performance in both patient care and standards of nursing.

Risk Manager/Nursing Supervisor

I worked as a risk manager/nursing supervisor in a 120-bed skilled care facility. However, the director of nursing did most of the reporting to the state. I was involved in reviewing all incident reports and sat on committees with the administrator, the director of nursing, and other department heads, which would make recommendations to improve and avoid such incidents from reoccurring. I sat in the administrative office on the weekends with representative from the attorney general's office who had come to the institution to investigate complaints they had received. They would state what they wanted to see. They never came outright and said what the complaint was, but based on the questions they asked, we would know right away what probably had happened. One particular family used to call the state repeatedly with unsubstantiated complaints. In one particular instance, the family had requested that the doctor and the nurse do certain things for their family member. A meeting was held with the director of nursing, and she promised the family she would follow through on their request. After the meeting with the family, the doctor was notified, and all of the family's complaints were addressed and documented in the patient's chart. Two days later, the patient expired, and the family claimed that we did not do anything for their family member and that we were the ones who caused her death. When the state investigated the matter, the institution was found blameless because everything had been done to save the patient's life. All doctor's orders were carried out, and everything that the family had requested was done.

The times I had meetings with the state on the weekends, they would ask for my name, title, and business card. They in turn would leave their business cards. I would give them the medical records that were available on the floor as they requested and answer all questions to the best of my knowledge. I would inform them that on the weekends the medical records department was closed, but that they could obtain the records on the next business day, either in person or by delivery. In my experiences with the state, wherever I was working, we were never, ever in immediate jeopardy of any violation of the state.

Another time, I was working on the weekends as the administrative supervisor in a180-bed skilled care facility. It was about dusk, and while I was on the second floor of the facility, a nurse asked me if I had heard the explosion. I had been at the other end of the building and did not hear it, but as I looked outside I saw fire in the direction she indicated. I immediately called the fire department, had the nurses keep all the patients on the floors, and had housekeeping guard the elevators on the first floor. I kept the visitors inside and notified the administrator and the director of nursing (DON). When the fire marshals came, they took over and told me what I should do. Everyone was directed to stay inside the building, and even when the DON and the administrator showed up, they were not allowed inside the premises. The patients and visitors were kept safe, and I kept the nurses informed as to what was happening. In the end, everything worked out well. Nobody was hurt, and I was commended by the fire marshal for following protocol.

Administrative Nursing Supervisor (Las Olas)

In my role as administrative nursing supervisor in a long-term care specialized hospital with ventilator patients, I was in charge of the 7 p.m.-to-7 a.m. tour. My responsibilities were great. The hospital was very busy at night with new admissions coming into the facility. Although it was small, the hospital consisted of an ICU, telemetry unit, and a medical/surgical unit. I gained a great body of knowledge there, in terms of making decisions, transferring patients in and out of ICU, initiating codes from respiratory and cardiac arrests, and continuing with cardiac resuscitation until the doctor arrived. In some cases, I was required to pronounce the patient's death after speaking with the physician and following the policies and procedures of the institution. I was involved in hurricane watches and warnings, and I participated in an actual evacuation of ventilated patients during a hurricane.

Nursing, as I mentioned earlier, is a calling because the overall responsibilities are great. While managing a long-term hospital on the night shift, in addition to all my nursing responsibilities, I had to go into the pharmacy and get medications for new patients that were admitted after the pharmacy was closed. To my delight, the state later prohibited the nursing supervisor from entering the pharmacy. The pharmacist had to come in if the medication needed was not in the medication box. This was a relief for me.

Running codes until the doctor arrived, transferring patients into and out of ICU, dealing with emergencies on the telemetry unit, and replacing sick calls often made it impossible for me to get a few minutes to eat. Yes, indeed, my job was demanding, but in spite of it all I got great satisfaction knowing that I was making a difference for all the patients.

Director of Nursing—Hospital

Being director of nursing for a small rehab hospital was another exciting experience for me. I was able to attend many conferences and was on several committees with doctors and other health-care administrators. These committees comprised the medical director, the administrator, the director of nursing, and other members of the health-care team. They focused on improving the standards of nursing care, including patient safety, updating the policy and procedure manual, infection control, pharmaceuticals, and improvements in rehab therapy. The focus of the committee was to ensure excellent patient care and recovery through nursing measures and physical therapy, and then returning the patient to a lower level of skilled care. In some instances, the patient would be discharged home.

Critical thinking was an important factor in becoming the director of nursing. I had to be prepared for a call saying the state was downstairs and wanted to see me. At times such as this, I would get the word to the administrator, all the nurses, and the CNAs that the state was in the house. In the few minutes before I went downstairs to meet the state's representative, I would make quick rounds to make sure that the medication room, the nursing station, and the medication cart had nothing that was out of compliance. I remember one day the gentleman from the state stayed with me for about three hours. First, he asked me for my business card, and he saw that not only was I a nurse but also a nursing home administrator; so he started to talk to me about his sister-in-law, who was also an administrator. He requested from me the current license for the pharmacy that we used and various agreements that we had with them. He did not stay in my office. Instead, he went and sat behind the nursing station while he reviewed all the documents. Most of what he reviewed was related to pharmacy. After he was finished, he asked to see the medication room. He looked at the carts, opened a few drawers, and looked in the refrigerator and checked the temperature. Before he left, he advised me on a few areas that we needed to update regarding the pharmacy that provided our medications, but we were not found to be in violation of anything.

I had to keep myself updated on all regulatory requirements that applied to long-term care hospitals. Part of the director's job was to be able to go through successful state surveys, audit charts, and communicate effectively with all the doctors and the health- care team in a professional and harmonious atmosphere. One of my main functions was to oversee the safety and quality of nursing care, in compliance with standards of the institution and the state. I had to adhere strictly to HIPAA guidelines, making sure that the staff complied with the strict standards of infection control. I was intimately involved with risk management and incident reports.

Staffing was very important to ensure that nursing and medical services were provided by competent professionals. The director of nursing had to review and update competency requirements for all employees who worked in the nursing department. S/he had to collaborate with the medical director, the administrator, and other practitioners to develop, implement, and evaluate policies and procedure that reflected the state's current standards of practice.

The mornings would start off with morning meetings. Once a week, there was an executive meeting before the morning meeting in which the medical director, the administrator, and the head of the organization would sometimes be present, along with many heads of various departments. They would talk about the admissions from the week before, the liaisons that went out to various acute care hospitals, and the doctors with whom they had conversations and made new connections. They would discuss patients who were potential admissions to the facility. They would discuss insurance, costs, and finances. After that meeting, there would be the regular morning meeting, at which the administrator, assistant administrator, director of nursing, director of admissions, director of social services, dietary director, director of physical therapy, maintenance director, director of medical records, and director of human resources, and any administrators in training that we had at the time. At these meetings, each service would report on their department, but the main department was the nursing department. The nursing department would report any deaths or transfers of residents to the acute care hospital during the night. They would report falls with injuries. They would report on admissions with complications or families with serious complaints.

At the meetings, we would review the number of discharges that were scheduled and the number of admissions that were expected. Social service would discuss problems that they might be having with the families in preparation for the patient's discharge. Building services might discuss problems that they were having with leaking from one floor to another, and the evacuation of that floor until the repairs were completed. The dietary department might report on patients who had lost weight or on patients who were not eating well.

Human resources might report that staff evaluations were not turned in, in a timely manner, or that some nurses had licenses that were due for renewal within the next month or weeks. Incident reports would be discussed and addressed. Depending on the season of the year, emergency preparedness would be reviewed in accordance with institutional policies and procedures as required by the state. The director of nursing is responsible for the coordination and planning of care for admissions and discharges, and coordinates emergency preparedness with the administrator. There would be frequent meetings with the administrator in disaster planning, covering fire drills, evacuation, flooding, bomb threats, and the like. Evacuation procedures and medication compliance in case of a disaster are reviewed often. Fire drills are conducted often to ensure that the staff is prepared for any such disaster. Staffing is planned and scheduled for before and after disastrous events. All staff members have to submit current working telephone numbers, and they are given a schedule to report on duty either before or after an event.

Each patient's chart had to be submitted to my office to be audited and completed before the charts were sent to medical records. Each admission that came to the institution was documented in a log with information such as where the patient came from, the patient's diagnosis, and whether or not the patient came in on antibiotics. If they were on antibiotics, what were they being treated for? This was an important part of tracking infections that might be coming into the institution from other hospitals. We also monitored infections that the patient developed while in our facility (i.e., nosocomial infections). Once per month, the infectious disease doctor would have meetings and go on rounds with the administrator, the director of nursing, the medical director, the head of housekeeping, and the head of dietary. The doctor would look at the physical setting and would randomly check different areas such as the pantry and the refrigerator, and would check the dates on the food and the temperature setting. The doctor would check for cleanliness and would walk into patients' rooms and inspect bathrooms, windowsills, and patients' drawers. She would go into the medication room and check to see if food items were stored in the refrigerator. She would go into the dialysis room and check various things, including the refrigerator, in that room. She also would visit the clean utility room and the dirty utility room. At the end of her inspection, we would sit and have a conference, at which time she would make note of her findings, make suggestions, educate us on the latest organisms causing infections, and update us on what was going on with the Centers for Disease Control (CDC) and other hospitals around the country.

Administrator in Training

I was an administrator in training (AIT) from July 1, 2006, through June 30, 2007; during this time I completed over two thousand hours of training and covered all the domains that are required in the state of Florida. I was successful in my state and national examinations, and since November 2007, I have been a licensed nursing home administrator.

My experience as an AIT was thorough, memorable, and valuable. I worked closely with the executive director of the nursing home, the assistant administrator, and the director of health information management (medical records). I learned a lot from each department, especially medical records. I audited more than nineteen hundred charts during that time. The director taught me many important things. Until this day, I will not start a note on the patient's chart unless there is the correct patient name and, most of all, the correct *medical record number.*

The valuable lessons I learned made me a better nurse and administrator. I consider myself privileged to have learned these lessons.

Conclusion

The nurse needs to have high moral standards and good character, and needs to be a critical thinker. S/he has to have a current license issued by the state in which s/he practices nursing. All her/his certifications have to be current. S/he must attend all mandatory continuing education classes in a timely fashion to keep her/his knowledge, competency, and skills updated. Nurses must attend seminars and become members of nursing associations, including those in her/his state as well as others, so that they can be versed in the latest regarding Medicare, Medicaid, the department of health, and the Centers for Disease Control. Keeping abreast of the latest technology and standards of practice from the state and the institution is vital. The nurse has to be a people person, one who wants to help others, and be compassionate and love the profession. Being understanding and nonjudgmental is very important. The nurse needs to be willing to comfort the sick and those who are afraid. When patients are taken to the ER, the worst things can enter their minds. Nurses are many things to many people, but to most patients they represent help and hope. Patients feel safer seeing a nurse.

Nurses constantly assess, prioritize, make decisions, delegate, call codes, and initiate CPR. Keeping abreast of technological developments is especially important today because most hospitals and nursing facilities rely on technology for nursing care. Today nurses have to be well educated to function competitively. Many nurses graduate with the bachelor of science degree in nursing and then go right into a graduate program for their master of science in nursing. Getting a higher degree makes them eligible to obtain a higher position in the organization where they work.

Some nurses get burnt out because they work too hard. Many nurses hold two jobs for many years throughout their careers. When they are off, all they can do is sleep. They spend little time with their families; however, most nurses try to do the best they can for their children by giving them a better education and a better life than they themselves had. Nurses need to recognize when nursing no longer makes them happy. They must stop and reassess their lives and find out if they need a change within the profession. Maybe they want a change from the area of nursing they are in. It could be that they don't want to work the floors anymore. They may want to work in one of the ICUs, administration, research, or home care. Maybe they want to do staff education, or become a clinician, supervisor, risk manager, or director of nursing. Many hospitals now refer to the director of nursing as the chief nursing officer. The nurse has to stop! Reevaluate your life; ask yourself what you really want to do with your life. What will make me happy? What will make me feel as excited as when I graduated from school or college? Once you get the answers, you many just need to work in a different area of nursing after completing the requirements for that department, or you may need to take time off and go back to school. Get the education that is required to achieve the goal you set for yourself. Talk with your supervisor, your family, and the director of your department. Maybe you have a mentor at work with whom you have a really good rapport. Talk to that person. Most of all, get your family on board and get started.

Nursing today is so diverse that you can work in many positions as a nurse—with the required educational qualifications—while still being the advocate that you want to be for your patients. Although education is important, experience is also very important. Most of all, you have to be happy with your job, because once the job is no longer satisfying to you, you lose your joy. With that loss, you cannot give the care and emotional support that your patients need. You have to be happy with what you do; otherwise, you will be miserable. Your supervisor will be unhappy, and your patient care will take its toll.

Making a change presents challenges, and for some people it's almost impossible to make the change that they need. Many nurses have financial hardships, not because of how much they earn, but because of their caring, giving, and nurturing nature. Nurses often support several family members, and over the years, these family members become dependent on them. On the other hand, some nurses balance their finances well. They make good investments, and when retirement draws near, they do not have to work because they need the money. However, some nurses cannot transcend their circumstances, because of the costs of higher education of their children, mortgages for homes they don't enjoy, and the expenses of cars that they hardly have time to drive. Some nurses have to help everyone else first before helping themselves. If you are one of these nurses, you have to be strong. Stop for a minute, prioritize, and assess your own situation just like you were assessing a patient. Think of what you need to do for yourself and what will benefit everyone in the long run. Once you come up with the answer, your attitude will change and your patients will appreciate you even more.

The goal of nursing is to provide quality nursing care to all patients through a collaborative effort that involves all disciplines from the health-care team. This care should be provided regardless of race, religion, or political affiliation. Most nurses go into the profession because they love people. They enjoy doing for others to help them get well. They are born public servants who want to make a difference by changing lives. They are dedicated and committed, and they take on a sacred responsibility not only to save lives but also to give hope, keeping patients safe above all things. They must keep abreast of the latest in the profession. They must attend conferences and mandatory in-services, and keep up with licensure requirements; CPR; advanced cardiac life support; and emergency preparedness such as fire drills, evacuation techniques, and general disaster preparations. S/ he must have great organizational skills and be a teacher to the patients, families, and nursing team.

I always have taken pride in my work as a nurse, and I still do. Spending over twenty years at Mount Sinai Hospital in New York City, I experienced and learned a great deal … lessons for life. I've met and worked with hundreds of patients and doctors over my thirty-eight years in the profession. Most nurses are a blessing to others. They really care. They feel good inside when they are able to make their patients feel happy and better about themselves. Some nurses love newborn nursery, others labor and delivery, others OR and recovery, others medical/surgical, and others dialysis, while there are others who like psychiatry, ER, or administration. However, wherever they work, they give of themselves and offer the best care in keeping their patients safe. Yes! Indeed, it's a calling from God to become a nurse.

Safety is the number one priority in caring for patients. It's not only preventing falls, accidents, and incidents. Safety encompasses everything that nurses do for their patients. First, there are the safety measures taken with the admissions process, the medications, the diet, and the activities that the patient can perform. It is the safety measures used in the nurse's assessment of each patient. Safety is needed in the documentation of medical records, for those patients on psychotropic drugs, and for those who are unable to verbalize their needs and are totally dependent on nursing care to live. Safety is caring for those who are confused, those with the tendency to elope, and those who have suffered a stroke but who refuse to accept the reality that they cannot eat regular food. They cannot accept that the swallowing reflexes have been compromised secondary to the stroke.

It's not just the state surveyors who should review the patients' clinical records looking for the safety nets put in place to avoid medical errors and medication errors. Safety is in the institution's policy and procedure manuals, and safety is in the laws and state requirements. The nurse, along with the entire health-care team, is responsible for collaborating in keeping all aspects of patient care safe. For example, the nurse and the pharmacists may discuss with the doctor from time to time whether or not a patient needs all twelve drugs that s/he is currently taking by reviewing the diagnosis and the medications that are being used for her/his particular ailments. It is the responsibility of the doctors, nurses, and the entire health-care team to note that the patient's appetite and food intake are poor while s/he is still taking all these medications. The nurse has a great responsibility placed on her/him, but s/he is the one who knows the patients best once they are hospitalized or in a nursing facility.

Safety is monitoring patients on anticoagulants. In auditing the charts, the nurse should say to herself, *When was the last PT/INR done? How much medication is the patient taking? Is the patient's blood too thin or too thick? Was the physician informed?* Safety is going to administer insulin to a patient and observing that he is cold and clammy. Immediately, you check his blood glucose and have glucagon on hand to administer subcutaneously if it is low. Or, if the patient is awake and alert, you administer orange juice immediately. Safety is observing a change in the patient's mental status. It is observing that Mrs. Smith looks different today. That's not how she usually looks. Safety is taking the vital signs, doing a finger stick, and getting results of over 500 mg/ dl—or even higher than the machine can read. Safety is making rounds only to find that the oxygen tank is empty, the patient looks pale, and the oxygen saturation level is in the low eighties. Safety means coming on duty, counting narcotics, checking the crash cart for the laryngoscope to make sure the light is present, the suction machine and the defibrillator are in working order, and the CPR board is on the cart. Safety is making sure all nursing procedures, medications, and treatments are documented on the correct patient's chart with the correct date and time, and the correct *medical record number.* It is monitoring all psychotropic drugs and following up with blood work.

Safety means preventing accidents and injuries by putting in place safety standards that can be measured and evaluated as to whether or not they are effective. Nurses are overworked in many cases. This is true for both hospitals and nursing facilities. The nurse gets blamed for everything that goes wrong. But if it was not for nurses, there could be no hospitals or nursing homes. Safety is making rounds after looking at the patients and their surroundings to prevent the spread of infections. Hand washing after each procedure, or several times during a procedure if needed, is important. Everyone knows that hand washing is the most effective way to prevent transmission of disease and infection. Safety is evaluating noncompliant patients and deciding whether or not to keep them on home-care service, or to notify the doctor, family, and insurance company and discharge them from home care.

When the CNA or PCA reports to the nurse that there is a skin tear or a hard, swollen area under the patient's neck or in his groin, and the nurse reports to the doctor and follows through, this is safety. Safety is active participation in fire drills on a regular basis at the institution where you work. Safety is giving the human resources and the nursing office your current and correct address and phone number. Safety is observing that the refrigerator for specimens (stool, urine, and wound cultures) is not located in the eye wash room, which is a clean room. It is making sure that all medications on the cart are not expired. Safety is checking that the pharmacist dispenses the correct medication and dosage as ordered by the physician. Safety is everything. It is controlling the spread of infection and needle sticks, preventing cross contamination, and disposing of blood and other body fluids properly. It is making sure that all nurses receive adequate orientation for the units on which they work. Safety is preventing patient information from being discussed on the elevator and at the lunch table. It is making sure that the director's office is locked at all times to protect sensitive information and narcotics that may be in the office.

Safety is reporting critical lab values to the physician as you receive them, and carrying out new orders given by the doctor. Safety is a discharge plan that includes all disciplines and considers the patient and her/his needs. Safety is having a written discharge order from the attending physician in charge. It involves the nurse who plays an important role in reviewing the discharge orders with the patient and caregiver. It involves reviewing medications with all discharge patients, especially the following: new diabetics; patients on anticoagulants; new dialysis patients; new transplant patients; and those with post-op coronary artery bypass grafts (CABG) and internal devices such as pacemakers and defibrillators. Port- A-Cath are usually for patients on chemotherapy. These patients should be given pamphlets on their specific diagnosis to follow up with the instruction. It involves making sure the patient has all emergency telephone numbers, including the number for the floor from which they are being discharged and the doctor's numbers. Most of all, safety is ensuring that the patient understands all the instructions and follow-up appointments with the doctors. Taking medications as ordered and following up with appointments can prevent unnecessary readmissions to the hospital. I have seen readmissions too often with noncompliant patients.

Safety is making sure medical records are kept safe from fire and floods, and that all medical records are backed up by the director of health information management and the administrator. Safety is making sure that these records can be retrieved whenever they are needed. It is keeping the medical records department locked at all times and making sure that only those who work in the department have access. It involves changing the codes as necessary, including when an employee is relieved of their duties in the institution.

The ultimate goal of nursing is to have the best and most dedicated, kind, caring, and understanding nurses who know that nursing care involves keeping all patients safe from harm and returning them to optimal health. In order to accomplish this, every employee from every department must work toward this goal: the administrator of the hospital or nursing home, medical director, doctors, chief nursing officers, pharmacists, social service, dietary, medical records, housekeeping, maintenance, and all other departments that are found in these facilities. That means, every worker in the institution is responsible for safety.

Appendixes

Testimonials

The following are some testimonials and endorsements of my performance over the many years of my nursing career. They are from doctors and nurse administrators with whom I have worked, and they show how these individuals felt about me as a nurse leader.

1. Most Outstanding Contribution to the Nursing Profession, June 13, 1971, graduation, St. Mary's Hospital School of Nursing, Rochester, New York

2. Sally Dirkowitz, RN, Assistant Director of Nursing, June 20, 1980, Queen's Hospital Center, Jamaica, New York

3. Ardean Lewis, RN, Assistant Director of Nursing, June 29, 1980, Queen's Hospital Center, Jamaica, New York

4. Evelyn Bersamin, Senior Associate Director, October 24, 2001, Queen's Hospital Center, Jamaica, New York

5. The Honorable Justice Diane A. Lebedepp, The Supreme Court of the State of New York, New York, New York, October 2001

6. Herschel J. Sklaroff, MD, PC, January 13, 2003, Mount Sinai Hospital Medical Center, New York, New York

7. Mrs. Sydney Prerau, Patient, November 2001, New York City

8. Alvin S. Teirstein, MD, Director of Pulmonary Division, Professor of Medicine, January 16, 2003, Mount Sinai Medical Center, New York, New York

9. Adrian J. Greenstein, MD, Professor of Surgery, January 22, 2003, Mount Sinai Medical Center, New York, New York

10. Cambridge *Who's Who Among Executives and Professionals in Nursing and Healthcare,* April 2007

11. Rosa K. Barksdale, CEO, Barksdale Homecare Services, Inc., October 13, 2008, New York

12. Diane A. Stone, Executive Director, June 4, 2010, Catholic Health Services, North Campus, Lauderdale Lakes, Florida

GRADUATION AWARDS

Saint Mary's Hospital School of Nursing Parents' Association Award for general excellence in nursing.

awarded to: CAROL M. FEKETE

Saint Mary's Hospital School of Nursing Alumnae Association Award to that member of the graduating class, who in the opinion of the Faculty, has demonstrated outstanding potential for success in and contribution to the nursing profession.

awarded to: JEAN M. DELL

The Doctor C. Stewart Nash Award for excellence in the art and science of nursing.

awarded to: JEANNE P. POWERS

The Saint Vincent de Paul Award, presented by the Daughters of Charity, to that member of the graduating class who has demonstrated marked devotion in her care of the sick.

awarded to: CATHERINE M. GAWLOWICZ

Saint Mary's Hospital School of Nursing Faculty Award to that member of the graduating class who has demonstrated outstanding personal and professional development throughout her course of studies.

awarded to: ROSALIE PUGLIESE

The Seton Award, sponsored by the Women's Board of Saint Mary's Hospital, to that member of the graduating class who, in her day to day interaction with people has contributed significantly to individual and group espirit de corps.

awarded to: ELAINE M. VANDUZER

The Student Association Award to that member of the graduating class, who in the opinion of the student body, has shown outstanding qualities of leadership and school spirit.

awarded to: ELAINE M. VANDUZER

Annual

Commencement

SAINT MARY'S HOSPITAL SCHOOL OF NURSING
ROCHESTER, NEW YORK

XEROX SQUARE AUDITORIUM

SUNDAY AFTERNOON
JUNE 13, 1971
at 3 o'clock

PROGRAM

Processional

Invocation
REVEREND JOHN V. ROSSE
Chaplain, Saint Mary's Hospital

SENIOR ADDRESS
PAMELA H. O'LEARY

PRESENTATION OF CLASS
VIRGINIA M. KRENZER
Director, School of Nursing

CONFERRING OF DIPLOMAS
MOST REVEREND JAMES E. KEARNEY, D.D.
Retired Bishop of Rochester

ANNOUNCEMENTS OF AWARDS
WILLIAM J. RIORDAN
Administrator, Saint Mary's Hospital

PRESENTATION OF AWARDS AND REMARKS
SISTER MARY WALTER
President, Board of Directors
Saint Mary's Hospital

PLEDGE OF FIDELITY TO DUTY

COMMENCEMENT ADDRESS
MOST REVEREND JAMES E. KEARNEY, D.D.

EPISCOPAL BLESSING
MOST REVEREND JAMES E. KEARNEY, D.D.

Recessional

Organist: Mr. Charles H. Wilson

Guests will please remain seated until
completion of the recessional.

GRADUATING CLASS OF 1971

President	BARBARA A. CURTIS
Vice President	CAROL M. FEKETE
Secretary	M. SHEILA JONES
Treasurer	LINDA A. SPANG

Heather Ann Barberio
Diane Louise Batz
Jean Bukiewicz
Noreen Catherine Charlebois
Barbara Ann Curtis
Christine Aukse Cypas
Karen Jean D'Agostino
Jean May Dell
Sharon Thompson Dragone

Sharon Kay Emerson
Mary Louise Enzinna
*Carol McCullough Fekete
Catherine Furcinito
Catherine Marie Gawlowicz
Margaret Mary Gilligan
Pamela Herrmann O'Leary
Denise Mae Hoover

Mary Sheila Jones
Martha Agnes Kirkey
Mary Louise LaVigne
Janice Lee Martens
Sandra Jean Moore
Beryl Lee Mulvey
Jeanne Phelps Powers
Rosalie Pugliese
Celeste Mary Ranaletta

Linda Ann Scialdone
Elaine Ann Serio
Teresa Agnes Sheeran
Kristina Zofija Sipaila
†Linda Whitney Spall
*Linda Anne Spang
Anne Marie Sweet
Elaine Mildred VanDuzer

graduated with honors
†*upon completion of program*

106

NEW YORK CITY HEALTH AND HOSPITALS CORPORATION

QUEENS HOSPITAL CENTER

82-68 164th STREET
JAMAICA, NEW YORK 11432

Affiliated with
LONG ISLAND JEWISH - HILLSIDE MEDICAL CENTER

HEALTH SCIENCES CENTER / S.U.N.Y. STONY BROOK

June 20, 1980

To Whom It May Concern:

I have known Jean Mc Grath since March 1978 when she joined
Queens Hospital Center as a Nursing Supervisor assigned to
the Surgical Service.

She made a rapid adjustment to the municipal hospital system
as to her responsibilities.

Her knowledge of the nursing process, labor relations and
decision making have been demonstrated to be above average.
In addition, she has cooperated with Nursing Service in
working additional tours to provide coverage for the Center.

In the discharge of her duties she displays a humane quality
toward both the employees and the patients without comprising
her professional responsibilities.

I believe she will be an asset to any organization.

Should you have any questions, do not hesitate to call me.

Sincerely yours,

Sally Pikowitz, R.N.
Assistant Director of Nursing

NEW YORK CITY HEALTH AND HOSPITALS CORPORATION

QUEENS HOSPITAL CENTER

82-68 164th STREET
JAMAICA, NEW YORK 11432

Affiliated with

LONG ISLAND JEWISH - HILLSIDE MEDICAL CENTER
CATHOLIC MEDICAL CENTER
HEALTH SCIENCES CENTER / S.U.N.Y. STONY BROOK

To Whom It May Concern

    Ms. Jean M. McGrath is a reliable person who can be depended on to perform her duties consistently well with little or no supervision. She works cheerfully and gets along well with other employees, showing pride and keen sense of responsibility in her work. Ms. McGrath accepts constructive criticism well and uses it well. She is presently attending school and attends continuing educational programs for purpose of continuous professional growth and development. As a supervisor of nurses, Ms. McGrath functions in such a way as to maintain a smooth functioning group.

Respectfully,

Ardean Lewis - 6/29/80

Ardean Lewis, R.N.
Assistant Director of Nursing

QUEENS COLLEGE
CITY UNIVERSITY OF NEW YORK
OFFICE OF GRADUATE ADMISSIONS
65-30 KISSENA BOULEVARD • FLUSHING, NEW YORK 11367-1597
(718) 997-5200 • FAX (718) 997-5193 • WWW.QC.EDU/GRADUATE_STUDIES

LETTER OF REFERENCE

To the Applicant:
Please complete *all* entries above the dotted line.

Print Full Name _JEAN Mc GRATH-BROWN_ S.S. # _____

Year and Semester of Expected Enrollment: ☑Fall ☐ Spring Year _2001_

Program of Study _Urban Affairs, M. A._ Program Code No. _348_

Name of Recommender _Mrs. Evelyn Bersamin, Senior Associate Director of Nursing._

I am aware of the rights afforded to me by the Federal Educational Rights and Privacy Act of 1974, as amended. I hereby ☐ do ☐ do not waive my right to examine the contents of this reference. I understand that by waiving my right I do so under the condition that the reference is used solely for the purpose for which it is requested.

Date _September 28th, 2001_ Applicant's Signature _Jean Mc Grath-Brown_

To the Recommender:
The student whose name appears above has applied for admission to a master's program at Queens College. This form is submitted to you for your evaluation of the applicant's qualifications both for graduate study and for a fellowship or an assistantship. Please tell us how long you have known the applicant and what you know about his/her academic ability, and include any other information that might make a difference concerning the student's application.

It is with great pleasure that I recommend Jean McGrath for admission to your graduate program in Urban Affairs.

I have known Jean professionally and personally over a period of many years. First, I worked with her in her role as a Supervisor of Nurses at Queens Hospital Center in 1988 and 1989. In that role, I found her to be a highly competent and conscientious staff member who applies herself with dedication, responsibility and energy. She has excellent knowledge base and broad experience which I observed consistently in her ability to conceptualize, provide leadership and work with others. As a supervisor, she had a

How would you compare this student with recent graduates in his/her field?

_X_ Upper Tenth _____Upper Third _____Average _____Below Average

Date _10-24-01_ Recommender's Signature _Evelyn L. Bersamin_

Recommender's Name and Title *(please print)* _Evelyn L. Bersamin, SR Associate Director_

Institution _Queens Hospital Center_

Please return this form to the student in a sealed envelope.

109

QUEENS HOSPITAL CENTER

New York City Health And Hospitals Corporation
82-68 164th Street, Jamaica, New York 11432
(718) 883-3000

Affiliated with
Mount Sinai School of Medicine

Letter of Reference Continued

multifaceted role that called for creativity, resourcefulness and practical
application of knowledge, all of which Jean exemplified well. Above all Jean
is highly motivated in achieving the goals she sets for herself.

Prior to the above position, Jean worked closely with other Assistant Directors
who found her to be dependable, committed and able to handle high level assignments which included providing administrative coverage for half of hospital
which has acute care services. She has served as an acting nurse administrator
and more than met the demands placed upon her.

The opportunity to pursue graduate studies will be an excellent avenue for
Jean McGrath to develop further and actualize her potential. Her keen ability
and fine personal attributes will be enhanced by the academic experience and
further study.

I am certain that Jeans maturity, tenacity and ability to do regular academic
work will enable her to succeed and do well in the program. The breadth of
her experience in health care and in her work with people will bring strength
and added dimension to her academic milieu.

QUEENS COLLEGE
CITY UNIVERSITY OF NEW YORK
OFFICE OF GRADUATE ADMISSIONS
65-30 KISSENA BOULEVARD • FLUSHING, NEW YORK 11367-1597
(718) 997-5200 • FAX (718) 997-5193 • WWW.QC.EDU/GRADUATE_STUDIES

LETTER OF REFERENCE

To the Applicant:
Please complete *all* entries above the dotted line.

Print Full Name _JEAN McGRATH-BROWN_ S.S. #

Year and Semester of Expected Enrollment: ☑ Fall ☐ Spring Year _2001_

Program of Study _Urban Affairs, M.A._ Program Code No. _348_

Name of Recommender _Mrs. Evelyn Bersamin, Senior Associate Director of Nursing._

I am aware of the rights afforded to me by the Federal Educational Rights and Privacy Act of 1974, as amended. I hereby ☐ do ☐ do not waive my right to examine the contents of this reference. I understand that by waiving my right I do so under the condition that the reference is used solely for the purpose for which it is requested.

Date _September 28th, 2001_ Applicant's Signature _Jean McGrath-Brown_

To the Recommender:
The student whose name appears above has applied for admission to a master's program at Queens College. This form is submitted to you for your evaluation of the applicant's qualifications both for graduate study and for a fellowship or an assistantship. Please tell us how long you have known the applicant and what you know about his/her academic ability, and include any other information that might make a difference concerning the student's application.

It is with great pleasure that I recommend Jean McGrath for admission to your graduate program in Urban Affairs.

I have known Jean professionally and personally over a period of many years. First, I worked with her in her role as a Supervisor of Nurses at Queens Hospital Center in 1988 and 1989. In that role, I found her to be a highly competent and conscientious staff member who applies herself with dedication, responsibility and energy. She has excellent knowledge base and broad experience which I observed consistently in her ability to conceptualize, provide leadership and work with others. As a supervisor, she had a

How would you compare this student with recent graduates in his/her field?

_X_ Upper Tenth ____ Upper Third ____ Average ____ Below Average

Date _10-24-01_ Recommender's Signature _Evelyn L. Bersamin_

Recommender's Name and Title (please print) _Evelyn L. Bersamin, SR Associate Director_

Institution _Queens Hospital Center_

Please return this form to the student in a sealed envelope.

HERSCHEL J. SKLAROFF, M.D., P.C.
1175 PARK AVE.
NEW YORK, NEW YORK 10028

(212) 289-6500
Fax 996-5042

January 13, 2003

To whom it may concern,

    Ms. Jean McGrath has asked me to write a letter of recommendation in her persuit of a new position in the field of nursing. Her credentials are impressive in their scope, allowing her to perform at a high level in almost any field of nursing.
    I have known Jean for many years at The Mount Sinai Hospital. She is very intelligent, hard working, enthusiastic, competent, accomplished and dedicated.
    I recommend her without reservation.

Sincerely,

Herschel J. Sklaroff, M.D.

112

Mrs. Sydney Prerau
20 East 74th St.
New York, New York 10021

To Whom it may Concern:

I have known Jean McGrath since November 2001 when I was a patient at Mt. Sinai Hospital in New York City.

From my experience with Jean McGrath as a nurse she is extremely competent, efficient and reliable in the execution of her profession. She has a broad knowledge of the content in her field. In addition, and perhaps most important I found her to be a very caring, understanding and sensitive person.

In addition, to Jean McGrath's academic nursing background and practical experience, She has a Bachelor Degree from Mary Mount College, Manhattan in New York City. There her major was Business Management. She is currently enrolled in a Master's Program in Urban Affairs at Queens College, New York.

It is indeed with great pleasure that I write this letter of recommendation.

Sincerely,

Bertha J Prerau

Martha Prerau

MOUNT SINAI
SCHOOL OF
MEDICINE

Alvin S. Teirstein, M.D.
Dr. George Baehr Professor
of Clinical Medicine
Director, Vivian Richenthal Research
Institute for Pulmonary and
Critical Care Medicine

One Gustave L. Levy Place
Box 1232
New York, NY 10029-6574

Tel.: (212) 241-5900
Fax: (212) 876-5519

January 16, 2003

To Whom It May Concern:

I am writing in strong support of Mrs. Jean McGrath, RN. I have known Mrs. McGrath for more than twenty years and have had the opportunity to observer her performance as a nurse and colleague closely. She is an intelligent, diligent, nurse and a delight to work with. She couples her knowledge and strong work ethics with a calm demeanor and ever-present smile. She has proven excellent leadership skill.

Mrs. McGrath has my enthusiastic support as an outstanding candidate to join your service. I would be happy to have her on my team.

Sincerely,

Alvin S. Teirstein, MD

Adrian J. Greenstein, M.D., F.A.C.S., F.R.C.S.
General Surgery
Department of Surgery

FAX (212) 534-2654
January 22, 2003

Re Jean McGrath

To Whom it may concern,

I am writing a letter to support the application of Jean McGrath for any future positions for which she may apply. I have known her since 1985. During this time I have had contact with her frequently on the wards, and she has taken care of a number of my patients. She is an experienced, competent and compassionate nurse. I have always found her to reliable, and hardworking. Her colleagues and other physicians have enjoyed her pleasant personality.
She has been exemplary as a nursing supervisor and is highly motivated in her professional work.
She is experienced in Medical Intensive Care, Surgical postoperative management, and Pediatric and Newborn treatment.
I would recommend her without reservation for any position in the medical field for which she may apply.

Yours sincerely,

Adrian J. Greenstein M. D., FRCS, FACS
Professor of Surgery
The Mount Sinai Medical Center

BARKSDALE MANAGEMENT CORP.
BARKSDALE HOME CARE SERVICES CORP.
BARKSDALE HEALTH CARE SERVICES CORP.

327 FIFTH AVENUE, PELHAM, N.Y. 10803 • TEL 914-738-5600 FAX 914-738-0858 • BRONX: 718-884-6700
E-Mail: Barksdaleceo@verizon.net • **Website:** Barksdaleathome.com

ROSA KITTRELL BARKSDALE
Chief Executive Officer

October 13, 2008

Re: Ms. Jean McGrath, (RN, MA, LNHA)

To Whom It May Concern:

Ms. Jean McGrath, (RN, MA, LNHA) has been employed as a consultant and nurse
educator for Barksdale Home Care Services, Inc for 3months.

We have found her to be a true professional as well as dependable. The feedback from
our staff about her continues to be positive and we enjoy working with her. She is a true
team player.

We recommend highly for any position she seeks. If you need to reach me for any reason
regarding this recommendation, please feel free to contact me directly
Thank you.

Sincerely yours,

Rosa K. Barksdale, Ceo
Barksdale Home Care Services, Inc
914.738.5600

Joint Commission
on Accreditation of Healthcare Organizations

Just A Call Away For Prompt Nursing Services

116

**ST. JOHN'S
REHABILITATION HOSPITAL
& NURSING CENTER**

3075 N.W. 35th Avenue
Lauderdale Lakes, Florida 33311
Tel: (954) 739-6233
Fax: (954) 733-9579

June 4, 2010

RE: Mrs. Jean McGrath: Administrator–In–Training Program
            Participated in an AIT program at St. John's Nursing Center.
            Located at 3075 NW 35th Avenue
            Lauderdale Lakes, Florida

To Whom It May Concern:

Mrs. Jean McGrath's Administrator-In-Training (AIT) program was from July 1, 2006-June 30th, 2007. She completed over 2000 hours and mastered all the Domains that are required in the State of Florida.

Mrs. McGrath completed many projects during her training one of which is still being used today. She created a RN/LPN Orientation and Competency Guide for all newly employed Nursing Staff to reference.

Mrs. McGrath also is a Registered Nurse which enhances her abilities as a Licensed Nursing Home Administrator.

I am a Licensed Nursing Home Administrator and Preceptor in the State of Florida.

Sincerely,

Diane A. Stone
Executive Director
Catholic Health Services North Campus

DAS: amg

Joint Commission
on Accreditation of Healthcare Organizations

Other Accomplishments

Some of the things I have done that are not listed in my resume are the following:

1. Recruited registered professional nurses from Jamaica, West Indies, for a hospital where I worked in the late 1980s

2. Volunteered for this same hospital, where I worked closely with a senior associate director of nursing before state surveys

3. Court-appointed guardian for an incapacitated person—position included a wide range of powers given to me by the court in the State of New York

4. Licensed private school director, University of the State of New York, Educational Department, December 6, 1993

5. Teacher, Hillcrest High School, medical paraprofessional (the late 1990s)

6. State survey visit at Mount Sinai Home Health Agency, August 15-19, 1991, recognition of home-care coordinator Jean McGrath

The Mount Sinai Hospital Home Health Agency

MINUTES OF PROFESSIONAL STAFF MEETING
New North Pavilion - Room A
100th St. & Madison Avenue
Tuesday August 20, 1991 -- 3:00 P.M. to 4:30 P.M.

Staff Meeting called to order by Joan Campbell, Director of Patient Services.

1. Minutes from last staff meeting were accepted.

2. Review of State Survey from August 15 to 19, 1991:
    a) 18 charts were reviewed
    b)   3 home visits made in the Manhattan and Bronx area
    c) variety of types of patients reviewed with multi disciplines
        involved. All records were very good with progress/problems clearly
        identified.

    f) Home Care Coordinator, Jean McGrath was identified as one of whose
        charts reflected the most complete and thorough follow up of
        identified problems.

Result of Survey - Satisfactory. Agency passed.

119

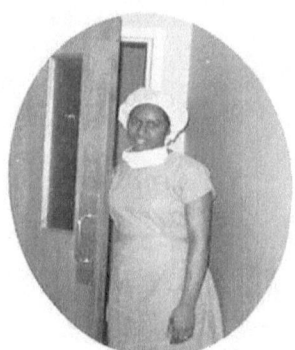

Dancing . . . eating . . . "Girls" . . . Toronto . . . T and
A . . . Airport . . . elephant . . . "Diamonds" . . .
cooking . . . Wedding . . . "I don't have anything to
wear." . . .

Jean May Dell
"Jeannie"

My Dear Friends,

When you receive your pin from St. Mary's Hospital on Graduation Day, you join a great group of nurses who, through the years, have brought prestige to your hospital. From that moment, you are "Children of Mary" in the finest sense of the word. When Christ said, "Unless ye become like little children, ye cannot enter into the Kingdom of Heaven," I'm sure he had in mind those who in years to come would choose His mother as their own. Your St. Mary's diploma makes you especially "her own." I know you will make His mother proud of you.

God bless you,
Bishop Kearney

Dedication _____

3

We, the class of 1971, dedicate
the final TRES ANNI to . . .

Past Graduates
Our Faculty
Arlene Minnamon

The most recent and final class at St. Mary's which graduated last Sunday.

MISS JOAN CARR, R.N.
B.S.N.

MRS. MARY R. MABIE,
R.N., B.S., M.A.
COORDINATOR

Medical Surgical
Instructors

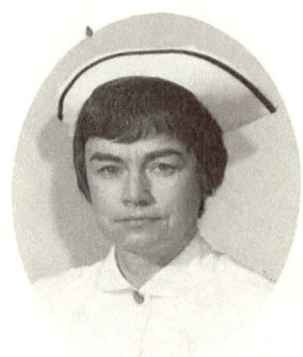

MRS. MARY SCHWALB, RN.,
B.S.N.ED.

MISS MARY MANION,
B.S.P.H.N.

Faculty of St. Mary's Hospital School of Nursing 1971

MISS MARY LOU MILLER
R.N. B.S.N. M.S.
COORDINATOR

MRS. ANNA MARIE KELLER
R.N., Dipl. of Nursg. Ed.

Maternal Child Health
Instructors

MISS HELEN FLEMING, A.S.A.,
B.S., Nutrition

MRS. BETTY KERR, R.N.,
B.S.N., B.A.

graduates

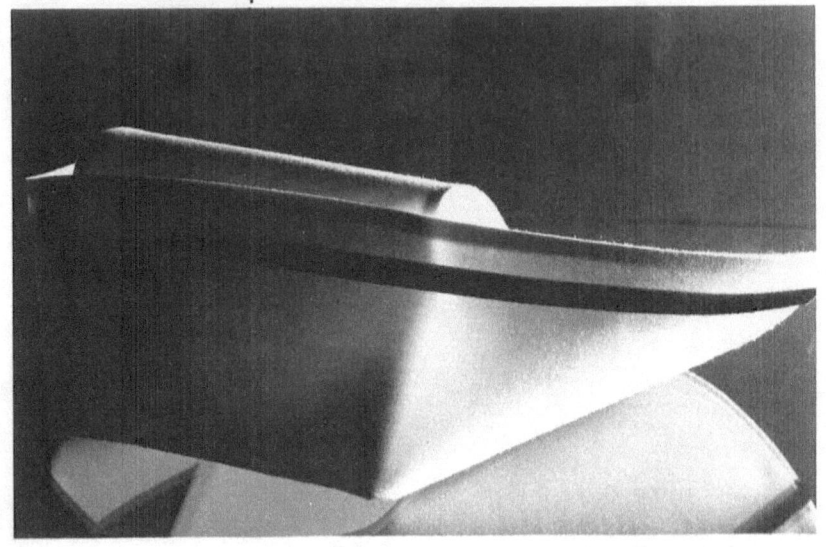

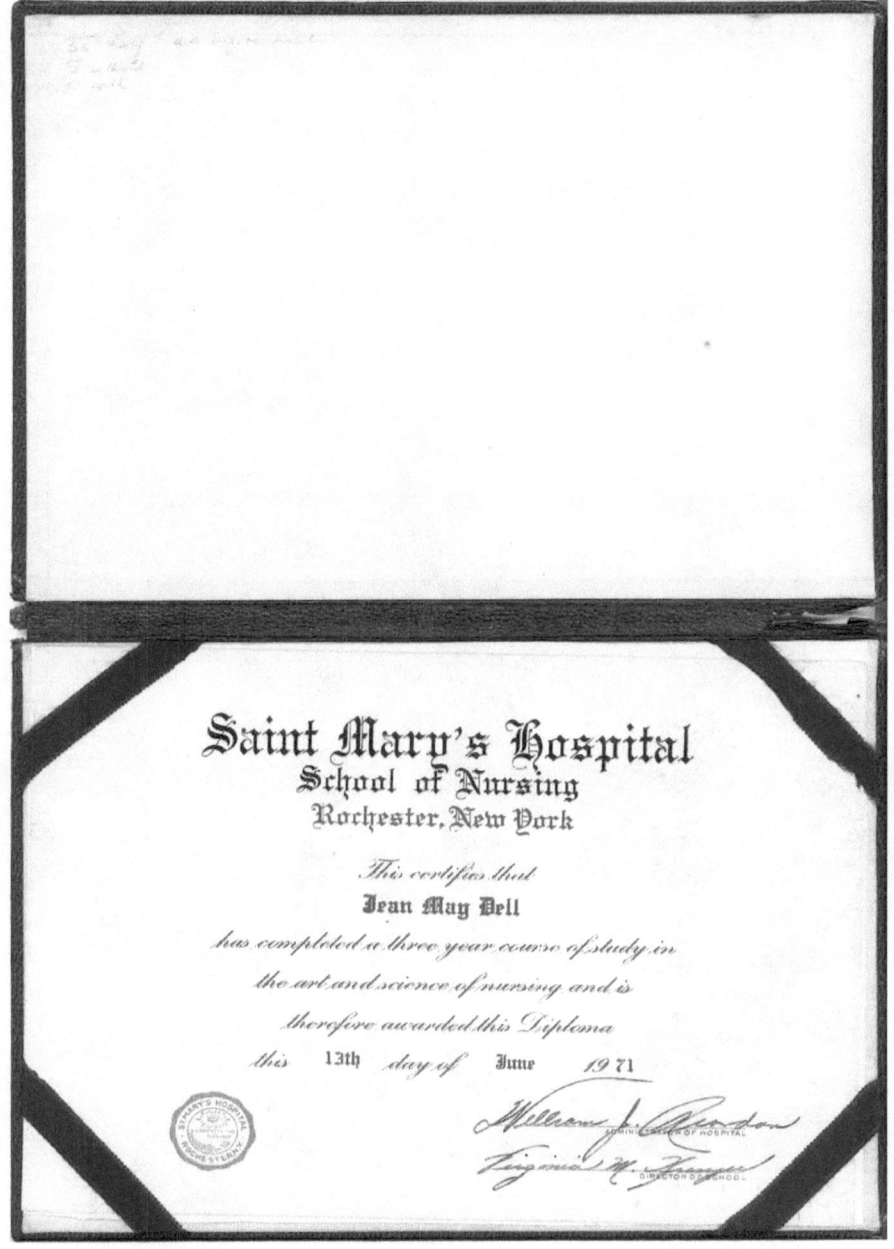

Saint Mary's Hospital
School of Nursing
Rochester, New York

This certifies that

Jean May Dell

has completed a three year course of study in

the art and science of nursing and is

therefore awarded this Diploma

this 13th *day of* June 19 71

William J. Reardon
ADMINISTRATOR OF HOSPITAL

Virginia M. Turner
DIRECTOR OF SCHOOL

James E. Kearney
Retired Bishop of Rochester

Joseph L. Hogan
Bishop of Rochester

Mr. Lionel Hampton, Jean McGrath, daughter
Susie, and granddaughter Taylor.

Degrees and Certifications

1. St. Mary's Hospital School of Nursing, Rochester, New York— three-year nursing diploma, June 13, 1971

2. Licensed in New York State, Florida, Georgia, Pennsylvania

3. Mary Mount Manhattan College, New York, New York— bachelor of arts, business management, June 1, 1982

4. Queens College, City University of New York, New York, New York—master of arts in urban affairs, June 3, 2004

5. Licensed nursing home administrator, State of Florida, Department of Health, Division of Medical Quality Assurance, Tallahassee, Florida, September 2007

Definitions

ADL   activities of daily living

AIT   administrator in training

CABG   coronary artery bypass graft. CABG surgery is advised for selected groups of patients with significant narrowing and blockages of the heart arteries (coronary artery disease). CABG surgery creates new routes around narrowed and blocked arteries, allowing sufficient blood flow to deliver oxygen and nutrients to the heart muscle.

CDC	Centers for Disease Control and Prevention
Cdiff	*Clostridium difficile,* often called *C. difficile* or C. diff, is a bacterium that can cause symptoms ranging from diarrhea to life-threatening inflammation of the colon. Illness from *C. difficile* most commonly affects older adults in hospitals or in long-term care facilities and typically occurs after the use of antibiotic medications.
CNA	certified nursing assistant
DNR	do not resuscitate
DNI	do not intubate
EMT	emergency medical technician
HIPPA	Health Insurance Portability and Accountability Act of 1996
ICU	intensive care unit
LPN	licensed practical nurse

moratorium	A period of time during which there is a suspension of admissions to a facility until the state determines an issue has been resolved and the moratorium is lifted.
MRSA	methicillin-resistant *Staphylococcus aureus* (MRSA) is a bacterium responsible for several difficult-to-treat infections in humans. It is also called multidrug-resistant *Staphylococcus aureus* and oxacillin-resistant *Staphylococcus aureus* (ORSA).
O2Sat	oxygen saturation
PCA	personal care assistant
PCA or PCa	patient-controlled analgesia—any method of allowing a person in pain to administer his own pain relief
PDR	*Physician's Desk Reference*—dictionary of medications
PICC or PIC	line A peripherally inserted central catheter (PICC or PIC line) is a form of intravenous access that can be used for a prolonged period of time (e.g., for long chemotherapy regimens, extended antibiotic therapy, or total parenteral nutrition).

RN   registered nurse

stat   immediately, at once

sundowning   a psychological phenomenon associated with
              increased

syndrome   confusion and restlessness in patients with
              some form of dementia. Most commonly
              associated with Alzheimer's disease, but also
              found in those with mixed dementia. The
              term "sundowning" was coined due to the
              timing of the patient's confusion. For patients
              with sundowning syndrome, a multitude of
              behavioral problems begin to occur in the
              evening or while the sun is setting.

TB   TB (tuberculosis) is a disease caused by the
              bacterium *Mycobacterium tuberculosis*. The
              bacteria usually attack the lungs, but TB
              bacteria can attack any part of the body, such
              as the kidney, spine, and brain. If not treated
              properly, TB can be fatal.

TPN	In total parenteral nutrition, a needle or catheter is placed in a patient's vein for ten to twelve hours, once a day or five times a week. TPN is used for patients who cannot or should not get their nutrition through eating. A patient's TPN may include a combination of sugar and carbohydrates (for energy), proteins (for muscle strength), lipids (fat), electrolytes, and trace elements.

U.S. Department of Health & Human Services

Improving the health, safety, and well-being of America

HIPAA Administrative Simplification Statute and Rules

To improve the efficiency and effectiveness of the health care system, the Health Insurance Portability and Accountability Act of 1996 (HIPAA), Public Law 104-191, included **Administrative Simplification** provisions that required HHS to adopt national standards for electronic health care transactions and code sets, unique health identifiers, and security. At the same time, Congress recognized that advances in electronic technology could erode the privacy of health information. Consequently, Congress incorporated into HIPAA provisions that mandated the adoption of Federal privacy protections for individually identifiable health information.

HHS published a final Privacy Rule in December 2000, which was later modified in August 2002. This Rule set national standards for the protection of individually identifiable health information by three types of covered entities: health plans, health care clearinghouses, and health care providers who conduct the standard health care transactions electronically. Compliance with the Privacy Rule was required as of April 14, 2003 (April 14, 2004, for small health plans).

HHS published a final Security Rule in February 2003. This Rule sets national standards for protecting the confidentiality, integrity, and availability of electronic protected health information. Compliance with the Security Rule was required as of April 20, 2005 (April 20, 2006 for small health plans).

OCR administers and enforces the Privacy Rule and the Security Rule.

Other HIPAA Administrative Simplification Rules are administered and enforced by the Centers for Medicare & Medicaid Services, and include:

- Transactions and Code Sets Standards
- Employer Identifier Standard
- National Provider Identifier Standard

The Enforcement Rule provides standards for the enforcement of all the Administrative Simplification Rules.

All of the HIPAA Administrative Simplification Rules are located at 45 CFR Parts 160, 162, and 164.

Bibliography

Centers for Disease Control and Prevention. September 13, 2012. Web, December 28, 2012.

Coronary Artery Bypass Graft Surgery (Heart Bypass Surgery, CABG). Information on MedicineNet.com. Web, December 28, 2012.

Department of Municipal and Community Affairs, Government of the Northwest Territories, RSS2, N.p., n.d. Web, January 25, 2013.

Education-Portal.com -. Web, January 25, 2013.

Florida Health Care Association. Nursing Home Administration. *Medical Errors: Prevention & Analysis.* Tallahassee: Florida Health Care Association, 2003. Revised, 2009. Print.

HIPAA Administrative Simplification Statute and Rules. Web, October 12, 2012. http://www.hhs.gov/ocr/privacy/hipaa/administrative/index.html.

Johnson, Tinisha. A Job Description of a Healthcare Risk Manager. *EHow.* Demand Media, May 22, 2010. Web, January 25, 2013.

Mosby's Pocket Dictionary of Medicine, Nursing & Health Professions, 6th Edition, Mosby Elsevier in affiliate with Elsevier, Inc., St. Louis, Missouri, 2010. Print (ISBN: 978-0-323-05291)

MRSA. Wikipedia. Wikimedia Foundation, March 30, 2013. Web, April 1, 2013.

PICC Line. Wikipedia. Wikimedia Foundation, November 10, 2012. Web, October 12, 2012. http://en.wikipedia.org/wiki/PICC_line.

St. Mary's Hospital School of Nursing, Rochester, New York. *Tres Anni* 1969 Yearbook; 1970 Yearbook; 1971 Yearbook.

Spiegel, Janet, and Noelle Shough, eds. *The Long-Term Care State Operations Manual.* Emily Sheahan (comp). Marblehead, Massachusetts: HCPro, 2007. Print.

Staff, Mayo Clinic. Definition. Mayo Foundation for Medical Education and Research, November 3, 2010. Web, December 28, 2012.

www.ingramcontent.com/pod-product-compliance
Lightning Source LLC
Chambersburg PA
CBHW031531120626
46545CB00005B/2101